Going Through Puberty

A boy's Manual for Body, Mind & Health

Going Through Puberty

A *boy's* Manual for Body, Mind & Health

Ruth J. Hickman, MD

Success within reach!

www.lessonladder.com
21 Orient Street, Melrose, MA 02176

Lesson Ladder/XAMonline, Inc., Melrose, MA 02176
© 2013 by Sharon A. Wynne (Text and illustrations)

Lesson Ladder: An Imprint of XAMonline, Inc.
21 Orient Street
Melrose, MA 02176
Toll Free 1-800-301-4647
Web: www.lessonladder.com
Illustrations: Beehive Illustration
Cover, interior design, and composition:
Delgado and Company, Inc.
Acquisitions editor: Beth Kaufman
Project management and production supervision:
Elizabeth A. St. Germain

Library of Congress Catalog Card Number:
(pending)
Hickman, Ruth. .
Going through puberty: A boy's manual for body, mind
and health. / Ruth Hickman.
90 pp., ill.
1. Title. 2. Puberty 3. Puberty—psychology 4. Parent and
teenager 5. Teenage boys
HQ797 H53 2013   612.661 H6286 2013
ISBN: 978-098- 844-9916

This book is intended to educate and provide general
information about puberty and child development. This
book should not, however, be construed to dispense
medical services or be used to diagnose or treat any
medical condition. All questions and decisions about
medical care should be addressed directly with qualified
health-care professional, including your child's pediatri-
cian. Accordingly, you are encouraged to consult your
personal health-care provider before adopting any of the
suggestions in this book or drawing inferences from it.

While the author, editor and publisher have endeavored
to prepare an accurate and helpful book, they make no
representations or warranties, express or implied, with
respect to the accuracy or completeness of its contents
and specifically disclaim any warranties of merchant-
ability or fitness for a particular purpose. The author,
editor and publisher do not assume and hereby disclaim
any liability to any party for any loss, damage or injury
caused, directly or indirectly, by any error, omission or
information provided in this book.

The names, conditions and identifying details of people
associated with the events and advice described in this
book have been changed to protect their privacy. Any
similarities to actual individuals are merely coincidental.

Published 2013
Printed in the United States
1 2 3 4 5 6 7 13 12 11 10 09 08

For all of today's girls and boys who will soon
become the young women and men of tomorrow.
Here's to your healthy growth and
development in all arenas!

Dr. H

Acknowledgments

The author would like to thank the following individuals
who worked tirelessly to make these books a reality: my
husband, Will Hickman, for reviewing early drafts of this book;
Sharon Wynne, President and CEO of Lesson Ladder; Elizabeth
Heller, Professional Writer; Kassi Radomski, Developmental
Editor; Beth Kaufman, Parenting Editor; Lisa Delgado, Interior
and Cover Designer, Elizabeth St. Germain, Production
Supervisor and Project Manager; the talented artists of
Beehive Illustration—Gemma Hastilow, Moreno Chiacchiera;
Bo Sherman, Director of Sales for Lesson Ladder; Dianne Liu,
Marketing Manager for Lesson Ladder; Anna Wong, Assistant
Editor; Nancy Brown, Editorial Assistant.

Above all, we would like to thank all the girls, boys, and
parents who gave permission to be interviewed and provided
multiple insights and quotes within these pages.

About the Author

Ruth Jessen Hickman, MD, has long been fascinated by questions of health, medicine, and life science. She is very proud of this book, in which she shares her knowledge with young adolescents.

Originally from Eastern Kentucky, Dr. Hickman graduated summa cum laude with a philosophy degree from Kenyon College in Gambier, Ohio. She developed an interest in neuroscience, so she pursued work at a neuroscience laboratory at The University of Illinois at Chicago and spent a year doing graduate work at the Integrated Biomedical Science Program at The Ohio State University. She then attended The Indiana University School of Medicine, from which she graduated with an MD in 2011. Since then, Dr. Hickman has worked as a health, medicine, and science writer, specializing in writing accurately and accessibly about medicine for patients and health science students.

Throughout her career, Dr. Hickman has pursued an interest in education. During college she volunteered as a tutor at local grade school. Later, during medical school, she volunteered with a group teaching basic medical concepts to fourth- and fifth-grade students, utilizing pictures, props, stories, and tissue samples. She noticed that these students were fascinated with the human body and eager to learn about themselves and how everything fits together.

Dr. Hickman became particularly convinced of the importance of quality patient education in the medical setting. She noticed that patients often had a poor understanding of their own medical conditions, and that this lack of understanding often contributed to poor health outcomes. She is especially excited about this most recent project because it provides her an opportunity to help young people feel comfortable and secure in their bodies. Since many health behaviors are established during adolescence, it provides a unique opportunity to encourage positive health choices over a lifetime.

Dr. Hickman is a member of the American Medical Writers Association. She has served as coauthor or first author on several academic papers. She has written for doctor's offices, patient-education websites, science and medical blogs, and medical education companies such as McGraw-Hill. She can be reached through her website, ruthjhickmanmd.com.

Ruth Jessen Hickman, MD

Contents

Part One

What Is Puberty? What Can I Expect?   1

Part Three

For Boys

Welcome to *Going through Puberty: A Boy's Manual for Body, Mind, and Health*. I'm Dr. Hickman, or "Dr. H," as I call myself in this book. I am a medical doctor who writes about health, science, and medicine. I am so excited about this book that I've written for you— young preteen and teenage boys who are or will be going through puberty. It is meant to be a helpful, encouraging resource you can turn to as you go through the ups and downs of puberty. In writing this book, I relied on my background and experience as a doctor to help you understand what happens to boys as they go through puberty. I also talked with many boys and young men about their experiences. Their thoughts are included in this book, too. You should understand that you are not alone. This can be a challenging time, but it is also an exciting time of growth and change.

How to Read This Book

Some of you may be excited to read the information in this book; others may feel nervous or embarrassed. You may feel a combination of emotions. Whatever you are feeling about puberty is totally normal. Take your time with this book. It covers a lot of topics, but you may still have many questions along the way. Don't be afraid to ask the adults in your life these questions.

What You'll Find in This Book

I have divided this book into three parts. In **Part One**, I cover the basic changes you'll be going through during puberty.

In **Part Two**, I talk about health and hygiene during puberty and beyond. This section provides a lot of tips you can use to keep yourself healthy.

It's not just your body that changes during puberty. Some of the biggest changes are in your emotions, thoughts, ideas, and feelings. I talk about these changes in **Part Three**. This section helps you understand these changes and gives you tips for putting together your new social and emotional puzzle.

Special Features

Throughout this book, you will find various special features:

- Boldfaced Key Words with definitions in the Glossary at the end of the book.
- It's a Fact! boxes highlight fun and interesting facts related to each chapter topic.
- Dr. H says provides additional insight or advice from the author.
- Quotes and stories from other preteen and teen boys, and occasionally from their parents, give you insight into others' thoughts and experiences.
- Just For Fun! gives you an opportunity to think and write about the many changes you're experiencing.
- Quick Quizzes are sprinkled throughout to "test" your knowledge. Don't worry, these quizzes aren't graded!

During the days ahead, at times you may feel more like a kid, and at other times, you may feel more like a grown-up. You might even feel like both at the same time! Whatever you are feeling, it's normal. It is an amazing time to be you!

Part One

What Is Puberty?
What Can I Expect?

uberty and **adolescence** are exciting times of growth and change in your body, your brain, and your mind. Puberty is a normal phase of development that occurs when a child's body transitions into an adult's body and becomes capable of reproduction. In this section, you'll learn what puberty is and read about the changes you can expect to take place in your body, your brain, and even your emotions. Later in this book, you'll learn what you can do to make yourself more comfortable with all these changes.

What Is Puberty?

Let's answer your questions...

- What Changes Can I Expect?
- Why Haven't I Started Puberty Yet?

What Changes Can I Expect?

Congratulations! You are beginning a new and exciting time in your life: **puberty**. Puberty is an exciting time of growth and change in your body, brain, and emotions.

Your Body

During puberty, your body will change in many different ways. This may seem strange. But these changes take place over months and years, so you'll have time to get used to it.

It's a Fact!

Boys typically start puberty around ages 9 to12. Girls start a bit earlier—typically around ages 8 to 11.

Body Changes

- Height quickly increases, then stops (called a **growth spurt**).
- Hair appears in places there wasn't hair before.
- Reproductive organs develop.
- Body proportions and composition change.
- Skin and hair may become oily.
- Voice deepens.

Hormones

Hormones are signaling molecules, special chemicals released into the bloodstream that travel all around your body. They help control how cells and organs work. While there are many different hormones in the body, two groups of hormones are particularly important for your development both before birth and during puberty: **androgens** and **estrogens**.

I call androgens "boy hormones" because boys have more of these hormones in their bodies. (Girls have more estrogens.) The hormone differences trigger the various changes that occur as boys and girls boys mature into men and women.

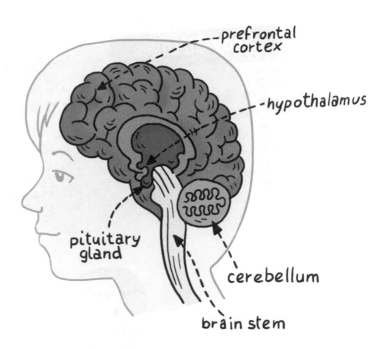

prefrontal cortex

hypothalamus

pituitary gland

cerebellum

brain stem

Your Brain

You probably know that your brain helps you think and feel. But did you know that even your brain changes during puberty?

Preteens and teens tend to:

- Respond to situations, especially emotional situations, more on feeling and intuition, while adults are more likely to use reason.
- Have more difficulty planning for the future than adults, although they are better at this than when they were children.
- Experience an increased drive for new and dramatic sensations. This is fine when the exciting experience is a safe one, like riding a roller coaster, but it can be problematic if the new sensation is unsafe.
- Find it harder to control that fun impulse and exchange it for a calm, logical look at the long-terms risks of a situation.

> My mom got her black belt in Tae Kwon Do when I was eight years old. It took me two more years to get mine than it did for her. I guess your brain might learn things better when you're a kid, but my mom showed me that you can still be young, even if you are old like she is."
>
> Oliver   age 11 (Mom was 41 when she got her black belt.)

Changes in Social Interactions

During puberty, parts of the brain involved in social interaction become more complex. Not only do social interactions become more complicated, but you also might become more sensitive to rejection by your peers. You might feel more self-conscious, and you might have more mood swings. All of this is related to developmental changes in certain areas of the brain.

Dr. H says: "One area of the brain that develops a lot during your preteen and teen years is the prefrontal cortex. This area is important for controlling impulses, moderating emotions with logic, and planning for the future. It won't fully mature until you are well into your twenties!"

I hate going to gym class because everyone is bigger than me. I still look like a little kid, and I hate it. Then I got clobbered at basketball practice last Saturday. My dad said to me after that when he was a kid, it seemed like he was the last boy to grow up. But in the end it didn't matter because he grew into a man like everyone else. Then he gave me some tips for playing against bigger kids. I didn't say anything, but it all made me feel better."

Jeffrey age 12

You May See the World a Little Differently

As the brain continues growing, it makes more connections among different brain areas. The speed of the connections among brain areas increases, too, contributing to more complex and abstract thoughts. You get better at looking at one situation and seeing how it is related to other situations. As you get older, you start to understand that not everything is "right" or "wrong," but that many situations are somewhere in between.

Stay Flexible Even if Your Brain Is Less Flexible

At the same time the brain is growing, it is starting to lose some of its flexibility. For example, some things are easier to learn as a child than as an adult, like languages. It is probably easier for you to learn a new language than it is for your mom or dad. This flexibility is one of the advantages of youth. You are still in the process of developing your self-identity, so it's easier for you to change than it is for adults.

Your Brain Doesn't "Make You" Do Anything!

It's important to understand that your brain doesn't "make you" do things. You always have a choice about how to respond to any situation. Knowing more about yourself and about how you are changing can help you make better decisions as you grow into adulthood!

Why Haven't I Started Puberty Yet?

Puberty happens at a different time for every boy. Once it starts, boys also differ in how long the process takes. This variation is normal. Just like some boys have blue eyes, and others have brown eyes, some boys go through puberty earlier, and others go through it later. Your body's timing is your own. Trust it!

Puberty Myths

You can't act like a kid anymore.

. . . .

You will suddenly be all grown up.

. . . .

All these changes will happen at the same time.

. . . .

Your body will be out of control.

. . . .

Your emotions will always feel extreme.

Quick Quiz

. . . .

The changes boys experience during puberty take place all at once over a very short period of time. True or False?

Just For Fun!

You just learned that the adolescent brain is not yet as good at planning or controlling impulses as the adult brain, that it loves thrills and excitement, and that it relies more on feelings and intuition than the adult brain. Can you think of any ways these differences might lead to conflicts between adolescents and adults? How might your perspective be different from the perspective of your parents, teachers, or coaches?

Changes in Your Body

Let's discuss changes in your body...

- Will I Really Grow Faster During Puberty?
- In What Other Ways Will My Body Change?
- How Do I Get Used To My Changing Body?

Will I Really Grow Faster During Puberty?

You've been gradually growing during your childhood. You may have experienced a few smaller growth spurts, but during puberty you really start growing. For boys, growth starts to pick up around ages 11 to 12. Most boys grow the fastest around age 13, but this varies a lot. Two or three years after your growth spurt starts, it starts to slow down. But you may still grow a little after that. By age 17 or 18, you will be close to your adult height.

It's a Fact!

Girls tend to get their growth spurt a couple of years before boys, which is why you may notice girls towering over the boys their age. But boys grow faster once they hit their growth spurt, and they keep growing longer than girls.

Body Parts Grow at Different Rates

During puberty, you might notice that not all of your body parts grow at the same rate. Your head doesn't grow much at all during puberty. Some parts of your body grow really fast, like your feet, legs, arms, and spine. What's funny is that your feet usually grow fastest first, then your arms and legs, and finally your spine. This can feel awkward for a while, but it's normal. It will all even out in the end.

Dr. H says: "Remember, all of these changes happen according to your own inner timing. There is no reason to worry if you are a little later or earlier than the average. Your body knows exactly what to do for you!"

It's a Fact!
At the peak of your growth spurt, you may grow four inches in a year.

In What Other Ways Will My Body Change?

Many boys are proud of another change: increased muscle mass. During puberty, the increased levels of "boy hormones" trigger muscle growth all over your body. You don't even have to work out to make this happen. It's your body's natural response. Your muscles get stronger and bigger, and they have greater endurance. You'll continue to get bigger muscles and increase your strength well into your twenties.

> Sometimes I feel like I can't get enough to eat. I could eat all day, and I still look skinny. I hope my muscles grow soon. My mom says she hopes so, too, because puberty makes keeping the refrigerator full really expensive!"

Ted age 13

Changes in Your Voice

One of the major changes people associate with puberty in boys is a deeper-sounding voice. This change doesn't happen overnight. It's a gradual process. Most boys notice their voice start to change around ages 11 to 15. This is usually just after the growth spurt revs up. Androgens cause your **larynx**, or voice box, to get larger. Your larynx is responsible for creating sounds when you speak. Your voice will become deeper over time, mostly due to the increased size of your larynx. Some boys' voices finish getting deeper

It's a Fact!

In most boys, the larynx grows so much that you can even see it sticking out from the neck a little. This is called an "Adam's apple." In girls, the larynx gets a little bigger, but usually not enough to see a noticeable Adam's apple.

by age 18 or so. But other boys' voices continue getting deeper into their twenties.

Most of the time, the deepening happens fairly slowly. You might not even notice it. Your voice might occasionally "crack" or "break" when its pitch briefly becomes unstable. Usually this happens when your voice is first starting to change, but it settles down after that. At the beginning, you might find it a little embarrassing when your voice cracks. But don't worry—it's all normal!

Dr. H says: "Try not to let these cracks and voice changes embarrass you. They are a sign that you are growing up, and soon you'll have your new voice. Your voice is more likely to crack if you are nervous, so try to stay calm and take deep breaths before you speak."

"I hated it when my voice started to crack when I talked—especially if it was in front of a girl. But girls didn't really seem to care, and it was happening to lots of guys in my class. So after a while, it just felt normal, and it really does stop doing that after a while."

Paul age 15

How Do I Get Used To My Changing Body?

It's normal to want to look and feel your best. As you go through puberty, and even as you become an adult, you might start focusing more on your appearance. This is normal! But sometimes this can get out of whack. You might begin to think too much about a single physical characteristic that you may consider a "flaw." For example, some boys worry about being much taller than others their age; others worry about being shorter.

It's best not to compare yourself to other boys. These changes happen to all boys, but they start at different times for different boys. Some of the boys who get their growth spurt later end up being the tallest adult men. The same is true about changes in boys' muscularity. Some boys bulk up a lot, and others bulk up less, even after they have gone through puberty. But don't sweat it! Your height and your size doesn't change who you are on the inside.

"I think guys are quieter about their concerns about how tall and how big they are. It is important for boys to remember that what really matters is who they are on the inside, not how they look on the outside. Bigger is not better. Smaller is not less. How you treat others is the real measure of how big a person you are."

—Daniel, father of two

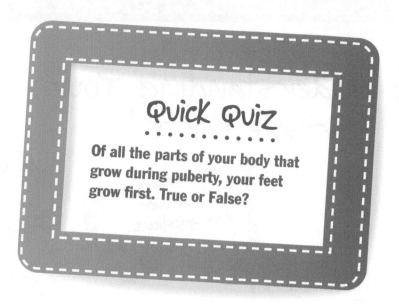

Quick Quiz

Of all the parts of your body that grow during puberty, your feet grow first. True or False?

Just For Fun!

DETERMINE YOUR APPROXIMATE Adult Height

If your parents are tall, you are likely to be tall. If your parents are short, you are likely to be short. There is a formula you can use to estimate your final adult height. But remember, your adult height may be somewhat more or less. First, add your father's height and mother's height in inches. Next, take that answer and add five inches to it. Finally, divide this number by two. The result is your approximate adult height.

For example, if your dad is six feet, one inch, you would add your dad's height in inches (6 feet × 12 inches in a foot = 72 inches) + 1 inch = 73 inches. If your mom is five feet, six inches, that is 66 inches. Now add the two together: **73** + **66** = 139 + 5 = **144** divided by 2 = 72 inches. Your estimated height is six feet! What number do you get for your approximate adult height?

Understanding Your "Private Parts"

Let's answer your questions...

- What Should I Know About My "Private Parts"?
- How Do My "Privates" Change During Puberty?
- What's the Difference Between a Penis That Is Circumcised and One That Isn't?
- Is It Okay If My Penis Gets Hard Sometimes?

What Should I Know About My "Private Parts"?

What you might refer to as your "private parts" are really reproductive organs: your **penis**, **testicles**, and **epididymis**. Your **scrotum** contains your testicles (also called **testes**) and your epididymis. Although you can't see your testicles, you can feel these round organs beneath the skin. During puberty, your testicles start to make two really important substances: androgens ("guy hormones") and **sperm**. The androgens cause most of the changes of puberty. The sperm travel along several ducts as they exit the testes and move up into the body. The first of these special ducts is called the epididymis. It feels kind of like a cord inside your scrotum. Several other glands make special fluids that dump into these ducts. Together, the sperm and these special fluids are called **semen**. Semen is released from the **urinary opening** of the penis in a process called **ejaculation**.

How Do My "Privates" Change During Puberty?

Your reproductive organs grew throughout your childhood, but during puberty their rate of growth increases. Growth of the scrotum and testicles is one of the first external signs of puberty. This first change can happen any time between ages 9 and 14. As the scrotum gets longer, the testicles enlarge and start to hang lower. The skin of the scrotum tends to darken as it gets looser.

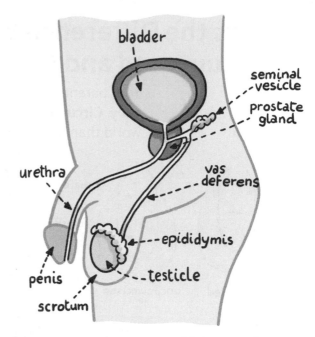

Male reproductive organs

A little later, the penis starts to grow longer and wider. Adult penises vary in size. Most guys will reach their adult penis size by age 16, but some will reach it before then. It is very common for preteen and teenage boys to worry about the size of their penis. But there are several reasons why you shouldn't worry.

- If you are still going through puberty, you haven't reached your adult penis size yet. Every boy's penis grows at a different rate.

- When you look down at your own penis, you see it at an angle, so it's easy to underestimate your size.

- It's inaccurate to compare size when the penis is limp. Smaller penises increase in size more than larger penises do, so you aren't getting a true comparison.

- Having a larger penis doesn't make a boy more like a man.

- A smaller penis is able do everything a larger penis can do.

- No one is going to judge you based on your penis size.

Quick Quiz

The testes produce androgens and sperm. True or False?

What's the Difference Between a Penis That Is Circumcised and One That Isn't?

Your parents chose whether to have you circumcised as a baby. **Circumcision** is more common in some parts of the world than others. Boys are born with a layer of skin, called the **foreskin**, which covers the head, or **glans**, of the penis. During circumcision, the foreskin is surgically removed to expose the end of the penis.

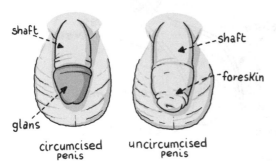

shaft

glans

circumcised penis

shaft

foreskin

uncircumcised penis

If you were not circumcised, your penis still has a foreskin. In most newborn baby boys, the foreskin cannot be pulled back over the glans and down the **shaft** of the penis. Over time, the foreskin becomes able to move a little more. At first, it just reveals the urinary opening. Later, it can be pulled over more of the glans. Boys vary widely in the time they reach these various stages. But eventually, the foreskin should be able to be pulled back over the entire glans. You can try to pull back the foreskin yourself, but be very gentle. Never force it to retract. Whether or not you are circumcised, your penis is able to do everything it needs to do!

It's a Fact!

Ever wonder why the scrotum and testes are outside the body? They don't seem very well protected there! The reason is that sperm production works best at temperatures a little lower than body temperature. Having the testes outside the rest of the body ensures that the sperm stay at the right temperature. This also explains why the scrotum moves up or down depending on the surrounding temperature. If it's cold, the scrotum contracts and brings the testes closer to the body, where they can warm up a little. If it's hot, the scrotum relaxes and hangs lower so the testes can cool off.

Is It Okay If My Penis Gets Hard Sometimes?

The penis becomes harder and firmer during an **erection**. This is completely normal. Ever since you were a baby, you've had occasional erections. But they start happening more often during your preteen and teen years. The penis is filled with with spongy tissue that has lots of holes in it. Normally these holes are empty. During an erection, the tissue in the penis becomes swollen with blood, which leads to a hard sensation. The penis starts to stick out from the body at an angle,

Going Through Puberty • A Boy's Manual for Body, Mind & Health

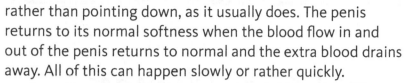

rather than pointing down, as it usually does. The penis returns to its normal softness when the blood flow in and out of the penis returns to normal and the extra blood drains away. All of this can happen slowly or rather quickly.

Sometimes you might have an erection after touching or rubbing your penis or when you think about something arousing. But at other times, the penis gets hard without either of these things. This is called a **spontaneous erection**. It can be a little embarrassing, but it is totally normal for all boys during puberty. There isn't a lot you can do to keep it from occasionally happening. You can make an erection less noticeable by wearing looser clothing, wearing briefs instead of boxers, or sitting down. If you are in class, you might be able to cover your lap with a sweatshirt or book. Spontaneous erections will occur less often as you get older.

Ejaculation

Sometimes, an erection leads to ejaculation. Very little boys don't ejaculate, but as you start to move through puberty, at some point you will have your first ejaculation. Sometimes when your penis is hard, you experience a very exciting and pleasurable feeling, known as an **orgasm**. Ejaculation happens during this pleasurable feeling. After ejaculation, your penis becomes soft again. About a teaspoon of semen is released as a thick, off-white or grayish fluid.

Sometimes a boy's first ejaculation comes when he is sleeping. This is called a **nocturnal emission**, or more commonly, a **wet dream**. If you have a wet dream, you may not even realize it until you wake up the next morning and find a wet, sticky place on your sheets. It is common for boys going through puberty to have wet dreams, but sometimes adult men have them, too. There is no way to keep from having wet dreams. If you don't want anyone to know you had a wet dream, volunteer to wash your sheets yourself.

> " The first time I got an erection at school I was sure everyone knew it, but really no one did. Don't stress about it. My dad even said that he once asked my mom if girls could tell this was happening, and my mom said she never noticed it even once during school. Just be cool and no one will know!"
>
> Arthur age 14

4 Hair and Skin Changes

Let's discuss hair and skin changes...

- Where Will Hair Changes Occur?
- What Is Happening to My Skin?
- Why Am I Sweating More?

Where Will Hair Changes Occur?

Other changes you'll see have to do with your hair. The hair on your head may change in thickness, texture, or color, and it may become oily.

Many boys notice their hair is oilier in their preteen and teen years than it was when they were younger. This is due to increased activity of **sebaceous glands**, tiny glands in the skin. These sebaceous glands release **sebum**, an oily substance that flows out onto the skin. Sebum is important to protect your skin and hair. But sometimes your body produces too much of it, and it ends up on your scalp. When this happens, many boys start washing their hair more often, which can help.

Quick Quiz

The texture or color of your hair may change during adolescence. True or False?

Changes in Body Hair

You will also start to see hair grow in places you didn't have it before. At first you will see just a bit of soft-colored hair at the base of the penis. The hair that grows here is called **pubic hair**. The appearance of pubic hair is often one of the first signs of puberty. There is a lot of variety in what this hair looks like. It often starts out thin and light-colored, but over time it usually becomes curlier and darker than the hair on your head.

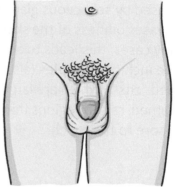

The appearance of pubic hair is one of the first signs of puberty

A year or two after the appearance of pubic hair, you will start to notice more hair growth on other body parts, too. Hair will start to grow in your armpits and on your arms, legs, and chest. Some boys grow hair on their backs and shoulders, too. Some boys grow a lot of hair, and others don't grow very much. You can get an idea of how much hair you will grow by looking at your dad and the other older males in your family.

Facial Hair

One other place hair growth will increase during your pre-teen and teen years is on your face. Many boys are excited to see their first facial hairs. Facial hair growth often starts around age 14 or 15, but it might be a little earlier or later than this. Usually a few light hairs start to appear at the corners of the upper lip. Then the hairs spread across the lip and become darker, coarser, and thicker. Later, the hair starts to spread to the upper parts of the cheek, to below the bottom lip, and to the sides of the face. When the hair growth becomes noticeable enough, you may want to start shaving.

> "I like having hair on my arms and legs, but I don't really want it under my arms and around my penis. It just seems weird. But I guess I don't have a choice."
>
> Tray age 11

What Is Happening to My Skin?

The increased sebum released by sebaceous glands increases oiliness of the skin. In many cases, this leads to **acne**. Acne includes **pimples** (also called "zits"), which are large, inflamed, raised regions that are sore to the touch.

Most young people experience at least a little acne at some point during adolescence. The most common locations for acne are on your face, neck, chest, and back. On your face, acne tends to be worse on your forehead, nose, and chin (called the "T-zone") because this area has the most sebaceous glands.

Going Through Puberty • A Boy's Manual for Body, Mind & Health

Dr. H says: "Almost everybody has to deal with acne at some point in his or her life. But there are many effective treatments. Later in the book you'll find tips for how to handle it."

Quick Quiz

· · · · · · · · · ·

You can only get acne on your face. True or False?

Why Am I Sweating More?

Sweating is an important way to keep cool. Once you enter puberty, a special kind of sweat gland is activated. These sweat glands release the type of sweat bacteria love. These bacteria don't hurt you in any way, but they do produce a waste product with a distinct smell that we call "body odor" or "B.O." Body odor is a natural and normal consequence of this cooling

Dr. H says: "There is a wide cultural variability about how much body odor is considered acceptable. In the United States, people tend to be very anti-body odor. But in many countries around the world, it is not such a big deal."

process. The funny thing is that you might not even notice your own odor, since it starts gradually, and you are always around the smell. But you might notice someone else's! No matter how much you sweat, don't worry about it! Sweating more is a natural part of growing up.

Part Two

Health and Hygiene

N ow you know about the most significant changes that happen In your body during puberty. In this section, I'll give you the information you need to deal with these changes effectively. As you grow up, you'll need to keep doing some things you are already doing to take care of yourself. But you may need to add to or modify your behaviors and routines. We'll also talk about some of the most important things you'll need to do to protect and promote your health as a preteen and beyond. Now that you're growing up, you're taking on even more responsibility for your health. The good habits you create now will take you into a healthy future!

5 Caring for Your Eyes, Teeth, and Ears

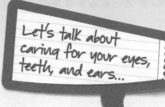

Let's talk about caring for your eyes, teeth, and ears...

- Why Do I Need Glasses?
- Do I Need to Brush My Teeth More Often?
- Can I Really Hurt My Ears?

Why Do I Need Glasses?

Vision problems become more common as boys become preteens and teenagers. During your growth spurt, your eyes grow very quickly, and sometimes one part of the eye grows out of proportion to the rest of the eye. When that happens, the eye can't properly focus on an image.

Changes in your eyesight often happen gradually, so you may not immediately notice a difference in your ability to see well. If you are having trouble making out objects, mention this to your parents, so you can get your eyes checked. Headaches or double vision are other signs that you may need to get an eye exam.

> I got scared one day because I noticed that some things were blurry far away. I was afraid to tell my mom and dad, but I did. I went to the eye doctor, and he said it was just strain from the computer. So now I am sure to take breaks from the screen while I do homework or play games. I guess I'm glad I got it checked it out."
>
> Charles age 11

Glasses

If you do have an issue with your vision, it usually isn't a big deal. Depending on your age, you will probably need either glasses or contacts. You may feel shy or upset about having to wear glasses. This is natural feeling. It may take some time to get used to them, but you will. Glasses are convenient to wear. All you need to keep them working great is a good lens cleaner. You can usually wear glasses comfortably while you are playing sports or being active outdoors.

Contacts

Contacts are another option for some people with vision issues. If you wear contacts, you have to be very responsible about taking care of them. Contacts can irritate or even infect your eyes if they are not cleaned regularly. If you do get contacts, be sure to follow all of your eye doctor's instructions.

Dr. H says: "If you feel like you are ready for the responsibility of contacts, you can mention to your parents that some contacts give sharper overall vision and sharper peripheral (side) vision than glasses. Some types may help keep your eyes from getting worse."

Protecting Your Eyes from the Sun

Even if you don't need glasses or contacts, every boy should invest in at least one pair of glasses— sunglasses! Even though your eyes don't get a sunburn like your skin can, radiation from the sun can damage your eyes. Look for cool shades that provide UVA/UVB protection. The sunglasses you choose do not have to be expensive to be effective.

Do I Need to Brush My Teeth More Often?

Just like when you were younger, you should brush your teeth at least twice a day. Your parents probably don't supervise your brushing the way they used to, so now it's up to you to do a great job even when no one is checking. That's part of growing up!

Pick a toothbrush with soft bristles, and make sure you replace it every few months. Dentists recommend toothpastes with fluoride to help prevent tooth decay. You can experiment with different brands of toothpaste to find one you like. Don't brush too hard! This can actually damage your teeth or gums. Hold your toothbrush at an angle to your gums. Make sure you brush the whole surface of every single tooth—it will take a few minutes. Don't forget to brush your tongue, too.

It is also important to floss daily. Flossing properly isn't hard, and your dentist can show you how to do it. While brushing and flossing daily can help prevent tooth decay and cavities, you should also avoid or limit your intake of sugary foods and drinks. Mouthwash with fluoride can provide extra protection if you are prone to cavities, and it helps keep your breath fresh.

Braces and Retainers

If your teeth grow in at the wrong angle or with improper spacing, you may need to have this corrected. Most of the time, this means getting a retainer, braces, or both. Retainers are used either before braces are put on your teeth or after your braces are removed.

Caring for Your Braces

It's easy for tooth decay to start behind your braces if you don't keep them really clean. So it's extra important to brush your teeth after every meal and every snack. It's even more important to floss your teeth regularly. Avoid hard or sticky foods that can break your braces.

Keep on Smiling

If you have to get braces, remember that they're temporary. In the meantime, use having braces as an opportunity to take really good care of your teeth. Remember, braces don't change the great person you are on the inside.

"Hey guys, believe it or not, parents can't stand telling you over and over again to do stuff like brush your teeth, floss, clean your braces, keep track of your glasses, and stuff like that. As you grow into young men, take responsibility for these things. Parents are more likely to let you do other things you want to do if you are showing responsibility at home."

—Matthew, father of two

Can I Really Hurt My Ears?

Dr. H says: "Don't forget to take care of your ears, too! Don't listen to your music too loud with or without earbuds or headphones. Over time, this can damage your hearing. If you can't hear what is going on around you while you are listening, turn down the volume! Also, even though it's tempting, don't stick anything inside your ears—not even a cotton swab. It's easy to puncture your eardrum that way. Finally, if you get your ears pierced, be sure to follow any instructions you get for keeping them clean. That will help minimize chances of infection."

It's a Fact!

The first pair of eyeglasses was invented in Italy in the thirteenth century. These glasses perched on top of the nose and had to be held in place with the hand.

Just For Fun!

Establish a New, Healthy Habit

It can take a while to establish new habits. Take some time to think about what healthy, new habit you want to establish for yourself. You may have more than one. When you choose a new habit, write it down. (For example, "I want to start flossing every day.") Then, make a plan for how you are going to establish this new habit. Reward yourself when you follow through with your new habit for a whole week!

Skin Care

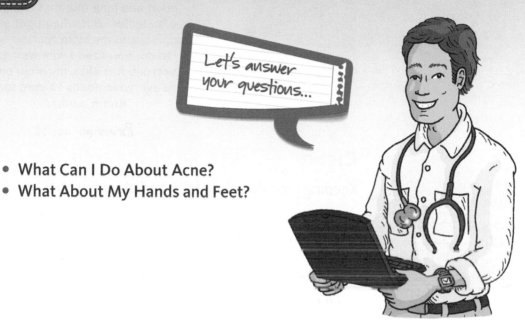

Let's answer
your questions...

- What Can I Do About Acne?
- What About My Hands and Feet?

What Can I Do About Acne?

Dr. H says: "If you are having trouble with very severe acne, you should see your doctor. There is no need to wait!"

Many preteens and teens struggle with acne. If you're one of them, you're not alone. Acne is highly treatable. If you are having problems with acne, first try the changes I suggest below. Give them a couple of months to work. If you are not satisfied with your results, see your family physician or a dermatologist (a doctor who specializes in skin problems). There are many effective treatments for acne that your doctor can prescribe. You don't have to suffer with acne. With good skin care and the help of your doctor, you can go through your teen years feeling happy in your own skin!

Skin Care Basics

There are three skin care basics:

1. Clean
2. Treat
3. Protect

> " I thought guys didn't really have to worry about their skin. I never saw any commercials for men about lotion and junk like that like you see for ladies. But when I got some pimples, and my mom told me what to do, I realized I was wrong. Everyone has skin, my mom said, and everyone needs to care for it! And it works."
>
> *Brennan* age 12

Clean

Keeping your skin clean is a good place to start.

- Gently clean your face twice a day with a mild facial-cleanser. There is no need to clean it more often than that. You can do this in the morning and evening. This will help wash away extra oil or dirt.
- Find a cleanser that says "noncomedogenic" or "nonacnegenic," which just means it won't aggravate acne.
- There is no need to use a harsh scrub.
- Use a gentle body wash or soap when you take a shower or bath and after you exercise.

Now that your face is clean, you'll want to try to keep it that way. If your hair touches your face, make sure you keep your hair clean, too. Oily hair can aggravate acne. Avoid tight-fitting hats, which can trap sweat, oil, and dirt. The same principle applies to body acne (usually on your chest or back), so avoid tight-fitting or dirty clothes. Change your pillowcase once a week. Also, try to avoid touching your face unless you have just washed your hands.

Treat

You can skip this step if acne isn't a problem for you. If it is, you'll want to apply some sort of treatment, usually after you wash your face. You can also buy a facial soap and body wash that contains one of these products, so you can clean and treat all at once.

- Start with an over-the-counter treatment. The most common products contain **benzoyl peroxide** or **salicylic acid**.
- Benzoyl peroxide works to kill the bacteria associated with acne formation. It is better than salicylic acid for treating pimples (acne that is red and puffy).
- Salicylic acid helps prevent clogged hair follicles and clean out follicles that are already plugged.

It can take a while for your skin to get used to these medications, so go slowly. They may cause your skin to be drier than usual. You'll want to buy a product you can use over your whole face (and any other area of your body where you have acne). You can also buy "spot treatments," which are usually more concentrated, to treat a painful, inflamed pimple. Some people have successfully used a combination of these products. Pick one product to start with until you see how your skin adjusts. If your skin has not cleared up after a couple of months, see your doctor.

Dr. H says: "Some people are sensitive to these products. So before using it on your face, apply the treatment to a small region of skin to make sure you aren't sensitive or allergic. Follow any package instructions carefully. If you use too much too fast, you may make your skin worse."

Protect

Protection is the final step for great-looking skin. You can protect yourself from the sun's radiation by wearing sunscreen every day. Over time, sun exposure can cause premature wrinkling, and it increases the risk of skin cancer. Skin cancer is the most common cancer in the United States, and it is the highest cancer risk for Americans 15 to 39 years old. Apply a layer of sunscreen every day after you wash your face and apply any acne treatment products.

The easiest way to apply sunscreen is to use a moisturizing lotion that has sunscreen in it. This way, you moisturize

and protect your skin all at once. Some over-the-counter acne medications and certain kinds of prescribed acne medications may dry out the skin, making moisturizer and sunscreen use even more important. Pick a sunscreen that says "full spectrum protection" or "protects against UVA and UVB rays." As with all products that go on your skin, if you have any trouble with acne, make sure you use a sunscreen that says it is "noncomedogenic" or "nonacnegenic."

Extended Protection

Of course, if you plan on getting extended sun, you'll need to apply sunscreen all over your body. Here are some tips for caring for your skin when you're in the sun:

- Don't forget to use a lip balm with SPF to protect your lips.
- Although the sun's rays are most damaging between 10 a.m. and 4 p.m., you need protection at other times of the day, too. You even need it in the winter and when it's cloudy.
- Use an SPF of at least 15. I recommend SPF 30, especially if you have fair skin.
- Make sure you use generous amounts of sunscreen, and reapply it often. Most people don't use enough sunscreen, so really slather it on any part of your body that will be exposed to the sun.
- Using additional protection like clothing and hats is a great idea, too.

Don't be fooled into thinking tanning is a safe way to get some sun. While it is true that a gentle tan is easier on your skin than a sunburn, even a tan damages your skin and increases your risk of skin cancer. In other words, there is no such thing as a safe tan. Your best bet is to slather on that high-SPF sunscreen before you catch some rays.

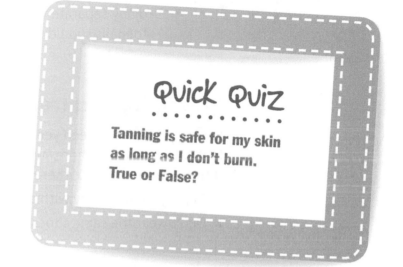

Quick Quiz

Tanning is safe for my skin as long as I don't burn. True or False?

What About My Hands and Feet?

You're old enough to know you need to wash your hands thoroughly with soap and water after you go to the bathroom. This helps prevent the spread of germs, which helps you stay healthy. Did you know it takes a while to properly wash off germs? You should wash your hands for as long as it takes you to sing the ABCs to yourself. You should also wash your hands before cooking, eating, or handling food. It's even more important to wash your hands frequently if you or people around you are sick. If you wash your hands a lot, you may need to use a moisturizer after you clean them, especially if they are already chapped and dry.

Nail Care

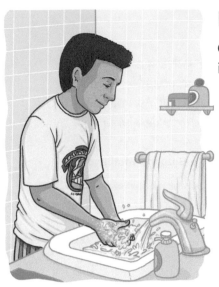

Germs love to hang out under your nails. So once in a while, you should clean under your nails by using one of the sharp nail cleaners that come with fingernail clippers. You can also scrub your nails with a clean (old) toothbrush and soap and water. Clip your nails regularly, too. Use a fingernail clipper and cut them in a slightly curved fashion down to near the end of the white part of the nail. Don't forget your toenails! You'll want to buy separate toenail clippers, which are larger. Toenails should be clipped straight across.

Preventing and Treating Foot Odor

During preteen and teen years, the sweat glands on your feet start producing more sweat. This can lead to stinky feet. If this is bothering you, there are a few things you can try.

- Clean your feet daily with an antibacterial soap.
- Don't wear the same shoes every day.

- Wear shoes that let your feet "breathe" more, not tight ones that make your feet sweat.
- Sprinkle foot power or baking soda inside your shoes to dry them out when you aren't using them.
- Put a dryer sheet inside your shoes at night to absorb moisture and leave a fresh scent.
- Don't wear socks and shoes all day. Give your feet a chance to breathe.
- If none of this works, try applying a layer of antiperspirant to your feet.

Athlete's Foot

Athlete's foot is a common problem in adolescence and adulthood, and you don't have to be an athlete to get it. Athlete's foot is caused by fungi, which are very small organisms somewhat similar to bacteria. Fungi love to grow in wet and moist places—even between your toes. When that happens, the area starts turn itchy, flaky, and painful. Anything you to do keep your feet and shoes dry will help prevent athlete's foot (and foot odor).

Athlete's foot can be successfully treated with over-the-counter medications, but see a doctor if you have trouble getting rid of it. To help prevent athlete's foot, you should wear flip-flops while walking in areas where the fungi can spread, like in public showers or at the swimming pool.

It's a Fact!

Your foot contains 26 bones; 33 joints; more than 100 tendons, muscles, and ligaments; and 250,000 sweat glands!

QUICK QUIZ

You have to be an athlete to get athlete's foot. True or False?

Q + A with Dr. H

Preteens and teens tend to have a lot of questions about acne. See if the Q & A with Dr. H. answers some of your questions. What other questions do you have about skin care? Write them down. If you don't find the answers to your questions in this book, be sure to talk to your parents or a doctor about them.

Q: *Is it ever okay to pop pimples?*

A: This is so tempting to do, but it is not a good idea. When you do this, you can introduce more bacteria and drive the infection deeper into the skin. It also makes it more likely that your pimples will leave scars. Apply a little spot treatment to the pimple and try not to touch it—it will go away soon!

Q: *I've heard that greasy foods may cause acne. Is that right? Do any foods cause acne?*

A: No specific foods have been proven to cause acne. Drinking plenty of water might help reduce acne, and an overall healthier diet may have a positive impact on acne. It certainly can't hurt!

7 Preventing Body Odor

Let's talk about body odor...

- **How Do I Prevent Body Odor?**
- **What About Deodorants and Antiperspirants?**

How Do I Prevent Body Odor?

It is pretty simple to keep body odor under control. To reduce body odor, shower once every day and right after exercising. Use a good soap that doesn't irritate your skin. There are a lot of different soap and body wash products out there. Here is some additional advice:

- Just like acne on your face, if you have acne on your body, you can treat it with a soap that has salicylic acid or benzoyl peroxide.
- Take special care to use soap under your armpits. Work up a nice lather, and use a washcloth.
- Change into clean, fresh clothes, socks, and underwear every day and after intense exercise.
- Pick clothes that will breathe well and allow some of your sweat to evaporate.
- If for some reason you can't shower after exercise, try to at least wash under your armpits with a wet washcloth (or use a paper towel if you don't have a washcloth handy).

What About Deodorants and Antiperspirants?

In addition to staying clean, you will probably want to use a **deodorant** or an **antiperspirant**. Deodorants have components that cover up body odor with a scent of their own. They may also contain ingredients that help inhibit the growth of bacteria, which decreases odor. Antiperspirants have a substance in them (aluminum) that actually decreases the amount of sweat that is released onto the skin. You can also buy a combination antiperspirant and deodorant.

There are many varieties and brands of these products available, so finding the kind you like the best may require some experimenting. You can also ask your friends who use them or ask your family members to see what they like and what works for them. Sticks, gels, and roll-on liquids are the most common forms of these products, but you can also get them in sprays, creams, and powders. See what feels most comfortable to you. You can try a variety of scents or try one that's unscented. Use it after you shower, or if you don't shower in the morning, apply it in the morning before you get dressed.

It's a Fact!

The ancient Egyptians may have been the first people to use deodorants. They used cinnamon and other spices for this purpose.

PLAN AHEAD

Take an outing with a parent or friend to the deodorant and antiperspirant aisle at your local drugstore. Choose one or two products you'd like to try, so you'll be ready when you need them.

8 Caring for Hair Up There and Elsewhere

Let's discuss hair care...

- How Do I Keep My Hair Looking Its Best
- What Do I Need to Know About Shaving?

How Do I Keep My Hair Looking Its Best?

You may not have given much thought to your hair in the past. Taking care of your hair now may be a little different from when you were younger. Because of all the amazing changes happening to you during puberty, your hair might have changed in texture, fullness, or oiliness. You may also be taking over responsibility for your own hair care and be making more decisions about your hair.

General Hair Care Suggestions

The specifics of your hair care routine will vary according to a your hair type and how you want your hair to look. Here are a few general hair care suggestions.

- Wash your hair regularly. Some boys may need or want to wash their hair every day. Keep in mind that washing your hair removes the natural oils, which actually help keep your hair shiny and healthy. At the same time, you probably don't want your hair to look like it is full of oil. Find the balance that works for you!

- Take care of your hair care tools. Periodically wash your brushes and combs in hot, soapy water and rinse them well afterward.

- Brush or comb your hair regularly. This distributes the natural oils in your hair and also keeps your hair tangle free and looking good.

- Find the right shampoo for your hair. Try out a few brands to see what works best for your hair.

- You might notice white flakes, called "dandruff," on your scalp. These flakes are actually dead skin cells caused by an inflammatory skin condition. Dandruff is common if your scalp is very oily. Often it can be treated with over-the-counter dandruff shampoos. Be sure to talk to your doctor if this doesn't help clear it up.

- Eat right. Good nutrition is necessary for healthy hair.

"I don't know why I did it, but I saw some scissors in the bathroom. I wanted to try to cut my own hair into this cool cut I saw in a sports magazine. It looked awful. Even the haircut lady couldn't do much to fix it until it got longer. Let someone else do the haircutting."

Lester age 12

QUICK QUIZ

Dandruff is most common when you have a very dry scalp. True or False?

What Do I Need to Know About Shaving?

At a certain point during puberty, you may want to begin shaving your face. Your hair comes in bit by bit, so when you first start shaving, you won't need to shave your whole face. You also probably won't need to shave every day. As more hair starts appearing on your face, you'll need to shave a larger area and shave more often.

Whether you shave is up to you. Some guys shave their faces, and some don't. It's up to you and your parents. However, keep in mind some schools, sports teams, and employers require a clean-shaven face.

Types of Razors

There are electric shavers and blade razors. Electric shavers don't require shaving cream, and you're less likely to cut yourself with an electric shaver. An electric shaver may be the best choice for you if your skin is easily irritated. The downside to electric shavers is that they can be expensive, and they don't give as close a shave. Blade razors can give you a closer, smoother shave. But it's easier to cut yourself with a blade razor, and they are more likely to cause irritation. If you use a blade razor, you'll need to buy shaving cream, too.

Following good techniques for shaving will decrease your chance of getting **razor burn**, an irritating rash that appears a few minutes after shaving. If you get razor burn, be sure to use fresh razor blades and plenty of shaving cream when you shave. Apply less pressure when you shave and shave in the direction of hair growth. You can also try using a soothing aftershave lotion.

Dr. H says: "**Razor bumps** are a kind of persistent irritation that occurs due to shaving. These bumps are painful and can look almost like acne. It is especially a problem for guys with tightly curled hair. The shaved hair curls back into the skin and causes irritation. If you are prone to razor bumps, you can buy special razors and aftershave products that can help, but ask your doctor if you continue to have problems."

QUICK QUIZ
. . . .
There is no way to prevent razor burn. True or False?

9

Caring for Your "Private Parts"

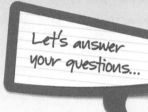

Let's answer your questions...

- **What Should I Know About Taking Care of My "Private Parts"?**
- **How Do I Protect My Genitals from Injury?**
- **What Is Jock Itch?**

What Should I Know About Taking Care of My "Private Parts"?

You should gently wash your genitals with a mild soap every time you take a shower or bath, at least several times a week. If you are not circumcised, pull back your foreskin as far as you can without forcing it, and clean the area. Your body produces a substance that helps the foreskin slide back and forth. If you don't wash thoroughly in this area, it can start to smell and can become a breeding ground for bacteria. Rinse the tip of the penis and the inside of the foreskin. Make sure you clean the area below the **corona** (the rim around the head of the penis). Don't forget to clean the base of the penis and the testicles, too. This is an area where smell can build up. If you experience any irritation, try washing the area with water only, or try a soap made for sensitive skin. Wear clean underwear every day, and choose underwear that isn't too tight.

Pain in the Testicles

You know the testes are very sensitive. If they get injured (which is common), you may experience significant pain. Most of these injuries will not need medical treatment. If you get hit in your testicles, lie down and apply an ice pack to the area. If the pain continues, you may want to take an over-the-counter pain medicine (such as ibuprofen). You should see a doctor if the pain does not go away within one hour; if you have bruising or swelling of the region; if you puncture the scrotum; or if you have pinkish urine, difficulty urinating, or continued nausea.

How Do I Protect My Genitals from Injury?

To protect your testicles, wear some type of athletic supporter, or **jockstrap**, when you are playing sports or exercising strenuously. A jock-strap has a waistband and a supportive pouch for the genitals. You can wear just a jockstrap for sports in which you'll be exercising heavily but are unlikely to be hit in your genital region, like gymnastics or running. You can also use special underwear and shorts for this purpose, as long as they support the testicles close to the body.

When you are playing sports in which your testicles might get hit, such as baseball or football, you should also wear a hard athletic cup. A cup can be worn with a jockstrap or with special briefs or shorts that are designed to hold it. The cup needs to fit tightly against the body. Jockstrap sizing is done according to waist size. Athletic cups come in sizes for boys, youths, and men. A salesperson at a sporting goods store should be able to help you find the right protective equipment in the right size for you.

What Is Jock Itch?

Jock itch is fairly common in adolescents and young men. It is not a serious condition, but it is uncomfortable. It is caused by the growth of a particular kind of fungus that thrives in warm, wet areas. Signs of jock itch include itching and pain in the area around the base of the genitals, thighs, and **anus**. You might notice red, scaly patches of skin. Usually the penis and the scrotum are not involved.

Jock itch is very common among male athletes, although any guy can get it. Using public showers and locker rooms increases your chances of getting jock itch. Jock itch can be passed from person to person by direct skin-to-skin contact or through contact with unwashed clothing. The fungi that cause athlete's foot also cause jock itch, which is why the two conditions often occur at the same time.

Preventing and Treating Jock Itch

Here are a few tips for preventing jock itch and treating it if you get it.

- Make sure you keep the area clean and dry.
- Wash and dry the area using a clean towel, and use a separate towel on the rest of your body.
- Wear clean underwear and other clothes.
- Apply an over-the-counter antifungal powder or cream according to the package directions.
- Make sure you also treat infections in other areas of the body, such as your feet.
- Don't wear tight-fitting underwear that irritates the area.
- Don't share clothes or towels with others.
- If you use an athletic supporter, wash it frequently.
- See a doctor if your infection lasts longer than two weeks or if you have recurrent or severe jock itch.

"I was embarrassed to tell my mom that my private area was really itchy. She finally noticed and got me some cream. I felt much better after I used it. Don't wait to tell someone if you are itchy down there!"

Steven age 13

Quick Quiz
. . . .
Only athletes get jock itch.
True or False?

10 Exercise

Let's talk about exercise...

- **What Are the Benefits of Exercise?**
- **Should I Take Exercise Supplements?**
- **Is It Possible to Exercise Too Much?**

What Are the Benefits of Exercise?

You've probably heard a lot about how good exercise is for your health today and in the future. This is absolutely true! It's good to get in the habit of exercising now, when you are young. You can take the good habits you establish now with you into adulthood.

Here are some of the ways exercise is good for your health:

- It lowers your resting heart rate, a sign that your heart is pumping more effectively.
- It helps prevent a number of health conditions like heart disease, diabetes, and arthritis.
- It burns calories, which is important for maintaining a healthy weight. When you combine healthy eating with daily exercise, you come up with an amazingly healthy you!
- It helps you deal more easily with the physical challenges of life because it helps build endurance and muscle mass.
- It boosts your energy levels, even when you aren't exercising.

- It can improve your mood and the quality of your sleep.
- It can be a great way to socialize if you exercise with others. Playing a team sport teaches other important skills, like the value of good sportsmanship and teamwork.
- It can help you feel more confident. This can be true if you practice long enough to get skilled at a particular activity, but also when you are just trying out a new activity. You become more confident when you prove to yourself that you aren't afraid to try new things!

Dr. H says: "Exercise is really anything that gets your body moving! It doesn't have to be a sport."

It's great that exercise benefits your health in so many ways, but exercise is also fun! If you don't think exercise is fun, it's probably because you haven't found the right kind of exercise for you.

The trick to exercising and sticking with it is to find one or more activities that you enjoy. Then it will be easy to establish positive exercise habits. Try to exercise at least a little bit every day.

Exercise Types

It's a good idea to try different types of exercise:

- **Cardiovascular activities (cardio).** Any exercise that raises your heart rate (like running, swimming, or biking) is considered a cardio activity. It gets the blood pumping through your body and increases your heart rate. This strengthens your heart and keeps you healthy.

- **Strength training.** This includes any type of exercise that exposes muscles to more weight than is typical. This strengthens your muscles over time. For example, you can do sit-ups to strengthen the muscles in your midsection, you can lift small weights, or you can do push-ups to strengthen your arms and shoulders. You should never try to lift very heavy weights—this can put too much strain on your developing muscles. If you want to try some strength training exercises, have a knowledge-able adult show you how.

Quick Quiz

Just walking doesn't really count as exercise. True or False?

- **Stretching**. Stretching your muscles is important when you exercise. Keeping your muscles loose and your body flexible helps prevent injuries. Yoga is one of the best types of exercise for stretching your muscles and learning a variety of ways to stay flexible. You can also do stretches as part of your warm-up or cool-down when you play sports or do other forms of exercise. Stretching also relaxes your nervous system, so it is a great way to stay calm and focused.

Avoid Being Overly Competitive

Everyone likes to win. Having the drive to be the best can be very positive. It can help you work harder and can motivate you when things get tough. But you don't want to get so competitive that all the fun goes out of the game. Some guys thrive on competition, but others don't enjoy it as much. If you have an especially competitive spirit, try to find a balance. You should be able to enjoy your sport even if you lose once in a while.

Should I Take Exercise Supplements?

There is a lot of pressure for boys to excel at sports by being bigger and stronger. Some boys think certain exercise supplements like creatine, protein powders, or herbs will help them with this. But there are many reasons you should stay away from exercise supplements. They may not be safe, and they may cause side effects. Even something that is normally good for you, like protein, can be harmful in excess. These products are expensive, too! You are better off eating a healthy and balanced diet.

Healthy Ways to Excel at Athletic Activities

No one needs to take supplements to do well in sports or athletic activities. There are many other things you can do to excel.

- Make sure you are getting enough sleep at night. Your muscles need time to rest and rebuild.

- Eat a nutritious diet. Optimize your fuel!

- Eat often enough. Make sure not to skip meals on days you have intense athletic activity. You may also need a snack before exercising.

- Stay hydrated when you exercise. Water is best, but you can drink sports drinks when it is extremely hot, if you are exercising for a long time, or if you are sweating a lot.

- Picture yourself going through the exercise or activity before you do it. Imagine yourself succeeding. This helps you get ready to perform your best.

- Avoid substances that can diminish sports performance, like cigarettes or other types of tobacco.

- Make specific training goals and stick to them. Keep track of your progress.

- Ask for tips from your coach, your teammates, or others who do the same activity you do.

- Keep trying new activities. If you find one activity or sport isn't for you, try another.

Dr. H says: "Many exercise supplements are dangerous, or their safety has not been proven, especially for young users. Just because a substance is legal doesn't mean it is safe. While it's understandable to want to improve your sports performance, most of these supplements are not very effective and may actually harm your health. Remember, there is no substitute for plain and simple hard work!"

- Have a balanced attitude. Try your best and focus on your strengths!
- Remember to have fun!

Is It Possible to Exercise Too Much?

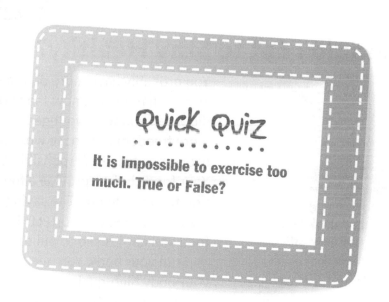

Overexercising is not good for you or your body. If you are participating in a sport, you shouldn't practice that sport more than five days a week. If you are practicing more than that, if you find you are frequently injured or sore, or if your muscles feel tired, you may be overdoing it. Sometimes boys exercise too much because they are trying to lose weight or bulk up. For some boys, exercise is all they think about most of the day. Talk to your parents or your coach if you are concerned about this for yourself or a friend.

Quick Quiz

It is impossible to exercise too much. True or False?

11 Nutrition

Let's talk about nutrition...

- **What Should I Eat to Stay Healthy?**
- **Dr. H's Guidelines for Healthy Eating**

What Should I Eat to Stay Healthy?

Dr. H says: "A nutritious diet helps you maintain a healthy weight, gives you energy to perform all your daily activities, and provides your body with the vitamins and minerals it needs to stay healthy."

You probably have more of a say about what you eat now than you did when you were younger. With more freedom to choose what you eat comes greater responsibility. Your food choices provide a foundation for your health. The saying "you are what you eat" is correct. The food you eat is used to build, repair, and run your body. You need to give your body high-quality fuel.

I've created a few simple guidelines for you when it comes to nutrition. If you follow these rules, you will be on your way to giving your body everything it needs to stay healthy!

Dr. H's Guidelines for Healthy Eating

1. Eat a balanced diet.

In other words, eat lots of different kinds of foods! This will help provide a range of **nutrients**, the chemical substances your body needs to survive and thrive. Each of these nutrients plays a different role in your body. Some nutrients you may have heard of are **carbohydrates** (which are in grains like rice or wheat bread), **fats** (like in olive oil or butter), **proteins** (like in meats, nuts, and beans), and **vitamins and minerals** (especially plentiful in fruits and vegetables). You need to eat a variety of foods to get all of the nutrients your body needs to be healthy. Eating too much of any one food at the expense of the others will make your body out of balance.

Go to www.ChooseMyPlate.gov to get an idea of how to structure your food choices to stay healthy. You'll notice there are big portion sizes for fruits and vegetables. The grain section provides most of the carbohydrates you need. The protein section provides your protein needs. The dairy section provides protein,

EVERYdAy FoodS	OccASiONAl FoodS
Baked potato	French fries
Yogurt with fresh fruit	Cherry pie or cake
Apple	Danish with apple filling
Whole grain bread with cheese	Crackers with processed cheese spread
Carrot sticks	Potato chips
Low-fat milk	Soda
Bran muffin	Doughnut
Whole grain pancakes	Sugary cereal

carbohydrates, and some important vitamins and minerals. Because most people get enough fat in the foods they eat, fat is not shown as a separate category.

2. Know the difference between everyday foods and occasional foods.

Some foods you could eat almost every day as part of a healthy diet. Other foods are better for special occasions. This does not mean a particular food is "bad" or "good." Above is a chart with some examples of everyday foods and occasional foods.

Here are a few more tips about everyday foods versus occasional foods:

- In general, foods that are very high in both sugar and fat (like most desserts) are occasional foods. Foods that are closer to their natural state are more nutritious than more heavily processed foods.

- Try to cut back on foods that have calories but no vitamins or minerals, such as soda.

3. When you are hungry, EAT!

Enjoy your food! You may find yourself hungrier than you used to be, especially as you are going through your growth spurt. You are going to need to take in more calories to support your extra height and weight. If you exercise a lot, you will need to eat to replenish the energy you use. Your brain needs good nutrition to go through all these changes, too. There's no need to count calories. Just listen to your body and respond to your hunger by choosing healthy everyday and occasional foods you enjoy.

4. Don't eat unless you are hungry.

Do you ever eat when you are bored? Do you ever eat in front of the television without even noticing or enjoying it? Do you ever eat because you are feeling a little sad or maybe even angry? A lot of people do this once in a while, but these are not good eating habits, and they can lead to unneeded weight gain. Here are some tips to help you pay attention to your hunger and notice when you are full:

- **Eat slowly.** Take your time eating. Chew slowly and pay attention to how delicious your food is. It takes your brain about 20 to 30 minutes to register that you are full, so give your body a chance to tell you that it's had enough.

- **Notice when you are full.** If you eat slowly and eat at a table with your family or friends, it is easier to notice this than if you eat in front of a computer or television. Sometimes food just tastes so good we want to eat more of it even when we are full. If this happens to you, try to remember to stop eating. Remind yourself you can have another serving tomorrow.

- **Don't overstuff yourself.** Eating too much feels unpleasant. Start with reasonable serving sizes. A serving size for a piece of meat is about the size of a deck of cards. The serving size for carbohydrates (like rice or mashed potatoes) is about the size of your closed fist. A serving of fruits and vegetables is also about the size of your fist, but you can usually eat fruits and vegetables without having to worry a lot about serving size.

- **Don't eat to feel good if you are upset.** Sometimes people eat when they are upset about something. They use food to distract themselves from their feelings. This is not a good habit. If you are upset or sad or concerned about something, the best thing to do is to talk to your parents or a trusted adult or friend.

"My mom told me to keep some granola and energy bars, the healthy kind, in my locker just in case I get really hungry during the day—which happens a lot. One day my friend was hungry, so I gave him one. Now he does it, too, and so do most the kids near my locker!"

Jack age 13

5. Have fun with food.
Food (along with clothing and shelter) is one of the necessities of life. We are so lucky that we need food to survive because food is delicious, and can it be fun, too. Try eating new foods and preparing foods in new ways. This is the only way to expand your food choices and find some new favorites.

6. Carry healthy snacks with you.
When you are growing, it can seem like you are hungry almost all the time! Take the time to prepare healthy snacks that you can have with you when you need them. This can prevent you from eating junk food since it won't be the only thing available.

7. Maintain a positive relationship with food.

Food is essential to a happy, healthy life! Sometimes boys develop an unhealthy obsession with their food choices by eating too much or not enough. In extreme cases, this can lead to eating disorders that require medical attention. Although eating disorders are less common in boys than girls, boys can develop them, too. Doctors rarely recommend a "diet" for preteens and teens. If you are unhappy with your weight, there are steps you can take to change it. Your doctor will likely suggest modifying your diet and exercising a little more, but you still need to eat lot of calories to be healthy. "Fad" diets and skipping meals can actually be dangerous. Never skip meals or try "dieting."

To be healthy and maintain a healthy body weight, you can choose fewer "occasional" foods and more "everyday" foods, only eat when you are hungry, watch your portion size, and get regular exercise. The most important thing is to be happy with the body you have. If you think you might have a problem with food, make sure you talk about it with your doctor or another adult you trust.

Healthy Snack Ideas

- Carrot and celery sticks with peanut butter or soy butter
- Low-fat microwave popcorn or packaged popcorn
- Trail mix (ingredients: one-quarter cup whole-grain cereal, raisins or dried cranberries, two tablespoons of sunflower seeds or chopped nuts (consider soy nuts), and chocolate chips)
- Low-fat plain or chocolate milk and whole-wheat pretzels
- Whole-grain crackers and string cheese
- Whole fruit (like apples, pears, or bananas) with string cheese or peanut butter, soy butter, or sunflower seed butter
- Mini-bagel with low-fat cream cheese
- Whole-wheat pretzels and turkey slices
- Baked whole-grain chips and salsa or bean dip

CAFFEINE

Caffeine is a substance found in coffee, tea, chocolate, hot chocolate, and many carbonated beverages like cola. Caffeine makes your body feel like it has extra energy. You should limit your use of caffeine to no more than one beverage a day. Too much can make you feel jittery or nervous. In very high doses, caffeine is unsafe for everybody, and even low doses can cause problems for those sensitive to it. If you feel jittery or are having trouble sleeping, cut back on your caffeine or eliminate it completely. Avoid energy drinks and other similar products completely. They have very high doses of caffeine, which can be dangerous.

Just For Fun!

TRACK WHAT YOU EAT

Pick a week (seven days in a row) and keep track of what you eat each day. Write it down on a piece of paper. At the end of the week, look at what you have written with your parents or even with your doctor. This will help you see where you are making good choices and where you might need to make a few changes.

12 Sleep

Let's discuss sleep needs...

- **Do My Sleep Needs Change as a Preteen and Teenager?**
- **How Can I Get Enough Sleep?**

Do My Sleep Needs Change as a Preteen and Teenager?

Your sleep needs change when you enter your preteen and teen years. Increased levels of hormones during this time affect the area of the brain that is responsible for setting your inner rhythm. This inner rhythm lets you know when to feel sleepy and when to feel awake. Your brain signals the release of a special hormone involved with sleep. As you get further into your teen years, this hormone is secreted later at night. Because of this, it may become harder to get to sleep early in the evening and wake up early in the morning. This pattern is completely normal, although it can be inconvenient, especially when you have to get up for school.

If you don't get enough sleep, it affects your health. You need enough sleep to be able to concentrate and learn well at school. Students who are sleep deprived can have trouble remembering information. Lack of sleep also can make you moody and less upbeat. In the long term, reduced sleep is associated with a greater risk of certain medical conditions, like diabetes. So it's important to prioritize getting enough sleep.

Sleep Needs

Many different factors affect how much sleep you need. Your age, stage of puberty, stress level, and level of physical activity all play a role. Some people need more sleep than others to function at their best. As a guideline, most preteens and young teens should aim for at least 9 to 10 hours a night. If you wake up in the morning without an alarm clock, you are probably getting enough sleep. If your parents have to drag you out of bed, you probably aren't getting enough sleep.

Dr. H says: "Some important hormones, like growth hormone, are released in greater quantities at night. So sleep is super important. Think about all the changes your body is going through during puberty—it needs to get enough rest to help you grow and change!"

It's a Fact!

Preteens and young teens need at least as much sleep as they did when they were younger and sometimes even more. Your sleep needs will start to decrease when you are an older teen.

Quick Quiz

Adolescents' sleep needs change due to increased hormone levels. True or False?

How Can I Get Enough Sleep?

With homework and perhaps one or more after-school activities, it can be hard to get enough sleep. Going to bed earlier can be challenging, since you may have a harder time falling asleep early than you did when you were younger. But getting enough sleep is a good habit you can develop.

Here are a few tips that may help you get the sleep you need:

- **Try to go to bed around the same time each night, even on weekends.** A lot of preteens and teens go to bed later on weekends. This is understandable, but it makes it even harder to fall asleep when you try to get back in your weekday pattern.

- **Make your bedroom a restful place.** You may want to consider studying, watching TV, or using the computer in other rooms of the house. Also, make sure your bedroom is quiet and dark when you go to sleep.

- **Have a bedtime routine.** When you were younger, you probably had a bedtime routine to help get you ready for bed. Now that you are older, you may want to create a new routine. Try to stop using any electronic devices (like your cell phone or computer) at least 30 minutes before bedtime. Instead, make a routine out of taking a shower, reading a book, listening to quiet music, or doing something else that relaxes you.

- **Assess your activities.** Some young people stay up too late working on homework because their other after-school activities take so much time. Of course, you need to get your homework done. Can you get some of it done earlier in the day? If you can't get to your homework until so late in the evening that you aren't get-ting enough sleep, you may need to think about whether you are involved in too many activities.

- **Exercise regularly, but not close to bedtime.** Exercise usually makes falling asleep easier, but it can make it harder if you do it just before bed.

- **Avoid eating too much right before bed.** This can make it harder to fall asleep. On the other hand, don't go to bed hungry or your growling stomach might keep you awake!

- **Avoid caffeine in the afternoon and evening.** Cut it out altogether if you can.

- **Is worrying keeping you awake at night?** Emotional upset can definitely make it harder to fall asleep at night. Remember, it is important to deal with your feelings! Try talking to someone you trust, like your parents or a counselor.

- **Sleep in on the weekends if you need to.** If you haven't had enough sleep during the week, you may need to catch up. It doesn't mean you're lazy! But you'll still need to try to get to bed at a reasonable hour.

> ❝ I like to get to sleep early. I always have. I get up early, too. My mom has to drag my big sister out of bed every morning, and she is always cranky."
>
> Dennis age 10

Cigarettes, Alcohol, and Drugs

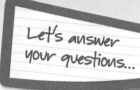

- **What Are the Health Risks of Smoking?**
- **Is Drinking Alcohol Ever Safe?**
- **What Are the Risks of Drugs?**

Dr. H says: "Lung cancer kills more men in the United States than any other type of cancer. Choosing not to smoke is a big deal for your long-term health!"

What Are the Health Risks of Smoking?

Plain and simple: Do not smoke. The health risks of smoking are very well documented. You will never have to worry about quitting if you never start smoking in the first place.

Not smoking is a powerful way to stay healthy during adolescence and into adulthood. Smoking increases the risk of multiple kinds of cancer, and it causes heart and lung disease. As people have learned more about the dangers of secondhand smoke, more public places have limited the use of tobacco products.

There are some immediate health risks of smoking:

- It makes your breath, hair, and clothes smell bad.
- It causes shortness of breath, rapid heartbeat, and impaired sports performance.
- It may cause skin to look pale and unhealthy.
- It can cause you to get sick more often.
- It can decrease your general energy level.

Many people who smoke started when they were teenagers, which is why you are likely to hear so many antismoking messages now. Fewer boys your age are taking up smoking these days, but far too many still do. The health risks of smoking far outweigh any immediate benefits you might get from it.

Many people seriously underestimate the addictive power of cigarettes. This is why the plan to smoke for a while but quit later is seriously flawed. You may not be able to quit later, or at the very least, quitting may be a big struggle for you.

Is Drinking Alcohol Ever Safe?

In the United States, it is illegal for people under the age of 21 to drink or purchase alcohol. Still, some teens experiment with alcohol, which includes wine, beer, and liquor. Alcohol is safe in small quantities for most adults, but larger quantities can damage multiple systems of the body. Someone who drinks too much alcohol at once can even die of something called "alcohol poisoning." It is also extremely dangerous and illegal for someone who has been drinking alcohol to drive.

At some point during your teen years, someone you know might pressure you to try some alcohol. Don't give in to the pressure.

Anyone who pressures you to do something you know isn't right is not your friend. Be upfront with your parents if you are ever in this kind of situation.

What Are the Risks of Drugs?

There are many types of illegal drugs, and they have many different effects on the body. Drugs can negatively affect almost every system of the body. Many drugs are highly addictive. That means that over time, a person needs to take the drugs just to feel normal. Drugs have many long-term negative effects, but they can also cause big problems right away.

As with alcohol, at some point, you may be pressured to experiment with illegal drugs. Rely on your best judgment and turn down the offer. If you like, think about some excuse. For example, say, "No thanks, I'm focusing on sports" or "My parents would kill me!" If the person offering you drugs is really your friend, then that should be enough.

Also keep in mind that not all prescription medications are safe. You should never take someone else's medication. Use your own good judgment, but be sure to talk with an adult you trust if a problem arises.

Quick Quiz

In the United States, drinking alcohol is against the law for anyone under the age of 21. True or False?

Plan Ahead

Planning ahead is often the best way to be prepared if someone asks you if you want to smoke, drink, or take illegal drugs. It can be easier to make positive choices about smoking, drinking, and drugs if you know what you think ahead of time. Sit down with your parents or another trusted adult, and come up with things you can say if someone offers you any of these substances. What would you say to someone who offered you alcohol or drugs? What if that person was a close friend? Would that change how you felt? Who can you turn to for help or guidance if this happens?

Part Three

Taking Care
of Your Emotions

In addition to the physical changes that you can see in yourself during this time, there are changes in yourself that aren't visible. You will spend the next several years growing up, exploring, and discovering who you are as person. It is an exciting time! You will probably start a new school. Some of your interests will change and expand. Your relationships with friends and family will change, too. You'll be forming new ideas about who you are and how you fit into the world. This section will help guide you through these changes.

Feeling Highs and Lows

Let's discuss emotions...

- Why Am I Experiencing More Mood Swings?
- Why Do My Feelings Seem More Intense?

Why Am I Experiencing More Mood Swings?

During adolescence, hormones go up and down a lot. This can contribute to **mood swings**. Life may seem a little more emotional or dramatic. Issues that used to be small might suddenly seem overwhelming. Everything feels personal. Sometimes you may feel at the top of your game, upbeat and positive, and other times you may feel down in the dumps. Your feelings may even go up and down in the same day! This variation is a normal part of growing up. Your moods will even out in time. Try to remind yourself that what you are feeling is part of adolescence.

Life Changes

It's not just that your hormones are changing—things in your life like school, sports or other after-school activities, family, and friends are also changing. Even positive change can be stressful. Maybe you have a crush on someone, and you're not sure how this person feels. Maybe you wish your parents would give you more independence, but they aren't sure you are ready for it. Maybe your parents are divorcing, or your family has money problems. Maybe you just won the state spelling bee and are on to the National Championship! Whatever is going on in your life can contribute to your mood.

Give Yourself a Break

It's important not to be hard on yourself when you are going through puberty and experiencing a roller coaster of emotions. The ups and downs you are experiencing are normal. Give yourself a break. Sometimes life and growing up feels stressful, but stress isn't always bad. Everyone experiences stress and has to find ways to properly deal with it. You can learn how to do that, too. Just give yourself time.

> " I don't like talking about feelings, and I don't know why my mom wants me to all the time. My sister loves to, but I don't. My dad said if I ever do want to talk, he will listen. That was all I needed."
>
> *Fuller* age 12

Why Do My Feelings Seem More Intense?

You may find yourself feeling your emotions more intensely than before. When you're angry or sad, you're really angry or really sad. This is normal during puberty. Our feelings often give us information about what's important to us and how we would like things to change. Below, I'll give you some tips for handling a variety of different emotions during puberty and beyond.

Feeling Angry

It's okay to feel angry. It's important not to stuff away your feelings. But it is equally important to express your anger and use it in appropriate ways.

- Let yourself cool down a little before you talk with someone who has made you angry.
- Take a few deep breaths and do something else for a little while. This makes it less likely you'll say something unfair or mean, which you might regret later. You can talk to the person who made you angry after you've calmed down.
- When you talk to the person who made you angry, describe what made you angry and how you would like to handle things in the future.
- Remember that name-calling and hurtful comments never make the situation better.
- Listen closely to what the other person has to say, even if you don't agree with it.
- Hopefully you and the other person can come to some sort of understanding, which will make things better the next time the issue comes up.
- Always try to end the conversation on a positive note.

Feeling Sad

It's normal for all of us to have down days. If something really bad happens, like a grandparent dies, it can take a long time to feel better. It is okay to take time to grieve. It's also natural to feel disappointed if you don't get something you wanted, like a part in the school play, or if someone you like doesn't like you in the same way. It's easy to get in a "sorry-for-yourself" mood. That's an okay place to be for a while, but eventually you need to learn how to make yourself feel better.

Consider these ideas the next time you are feeling sad:

- **Give yourself a time limit.** Allow yourself to feel really, super sad for 20 minutes. Set a timer and go ahead and let yourself be blue. When the time is up, move on to something you enjoy doing for at least an hour. If you feel like you want to be sad again, remind yourself that you have to wait until the hour is up. Most of the time, you will forget your sadness and just feel better!

- **Stay busy.** Go for a walk, call a friend, talk to your sister or brother, or play with your dog. Do something to get your mind on what makes you happy.

- **Make lists.** When you are feeling happy, make a list of things you love to do that make you feel good. When you are sad, check the list and do one of those things.

- **Talk to someone.** Talking to a friend or parent is a great way to share your feelings and get support. Talking about what is bothering you (or just talking about the fact that you aren't sure why you feel so sad) is a great way to feel better.

- **Laugh!** Read a joke book, call a funny friend, or watch a silly video or movie. Or just force yourself to laugh at nothing. After a few minutes of laughing, your whole body and mind will feel better!

Feeling Anxious

Anxiety, or very nervous feelings, can be another challenging emotion to handle. **Stress**, especially stress you are not aware of, can cause anxiety. Things like talking to someone you like, starting a new school, taking a big test, or performing in the school play can also produce nervous feelings. These situations may make your palms sweat and make your heart beat faster. A little anxiety is often a good thing—it gets us primed and ready for action. But anxiety can be a problem if it starts to happen too often, or if it does not seem to go away. If anxiety is keeping you from doing the things you'd like to do, you should talk to your parents and your doctor to find ways to help you feel better and more relaxed.

Feeling Self-Conscious

Almost everyone feels more **self-conscious** while they are going through puberty. There are so many changes happening in your body and in your life that you may feel like everyone is noticing everything about you. Sometimes it might feel as if a spotlight is on you all the time. You may think about your actions over and over. You may worry about how other people will respond to what you say or do. You may feel easily embarrassed, or you may worry too much about how other people feel about you.

While it's normal to be more self-conscious as you go through puberty, you don't want what other people think (or what you think they think) to direct your actions or feelings. Try not to worry too much about what others think of you. As you work on building your self-esteem, you will become less self-conscious.

Dr. H says: "It is important for you to be who you are, and do the things you love, no matter what other people might think."

Getting Help If You Need It

Anger, sadness, and anxiety that go beyond normal limits can hold you back and keep you from being the best you can be. Exercising, eating well, sleeping enough, and taking deep breaths can help balance your emotions. However, there may still be times when these emotions are too much to deal with on your own.

Dr. H says: "If you feel so bad that you are worried you might hurt yourself in any way, be sure to tell an adult, so you can get help right away. You should do the same for a friend you are really worried about."

If you feel like your emotions are overwhelming, you should talk with someone who cares about you (like a parent, your doctor, or another trusted adult). You might also want to ask your parents if you can talk with a professional counselor or therapist. Your school might have a psychologist or social worker you can talk to about how you're feeling—especially if it's getting in the way of your ability to concentrate and do well at school. Sometimes having a person to talk to who is there just for you is a great way to get yourself feeling back to normal.

Feeling Happy

During puberty, you will also have many awesome, positive feelings and experiences that are special and memorable, like scoring a winning goal, going out with someone special, getting straight A's on a report card, taking a fun trip with your family or friends, and more! Even your positive feelings will be more intense during adolescence. You will have a lot of happy feelings that you will remember with special fondness as you get older.

> ### Just For Fun!
>
> ### Make a Happy List
>
> Write down a list of at least 10 things you can do that make you feel happy. For example: Play sports, watch your favorite movie, go for a walk with your dog, play video games with a friend, call one of your favorite relatives, do an art project, read your favorite book, or listen to your favorite music. Once you have a list, keep it handy for the next time you need to boost your mood. Pick one of the things on your list and do it. Then see if you feel better!

15 Self-Esteem

Let's talk about self-esteem...

- How Do I Build My Self-Esteem?
- How Do I Deal with Bullies?

Dr. H says: "Self-esteem refers to a person's self-regard—how he thinks and feels about himself. It's a measure of a person's self-respect. Having a strong self-esteem means valuing your own worth and taking pride in who you are."

How Do I Build My Self-Esteem?

Self-esteem is like the foundation of a house. If it is strong, the house will be sturdy and able to weather storms and strong winds. If the foundation is weak, the house is at risk of falling down or crumbling when the weather gets rough. Your self-esteem is the foundation of you! If you love yourself and respect yourself, then you will have a strong base during the sometimes-rocky path of your preteen and teen years—and throughout your adult life.

Poor Self-Esteem

Having poor self-esteem can make it harder to make good choices for yourself. If you don't respect yourself, it is easier for other people to influence you and your decisions. Some of these people may not have your best interests at heart. Poor self-esteem can make you less confident and less likely to try new things. If you are less confident, it's harder for you to take on new challenges and succeed at them, which can help to build self-esteem. When you feel like you aren't worth anything, you often start to treat yourself like that. Other people might begin to treat you that way, too.

"I had a bad game once at basketball. One of my teammates said I blew the game, and I shouldn't play anymore. I believed him. I kept going to practice but I played really bad. My dad saw one day when he came to pick me up. On the way home, he asked me if something was wrong. I didn't really want to talk about it, but I finally did. He said that it was ridiculous. Everyone, including NBA stars, have bad games. When you are on a team, you win and lose as a team. He said you can't listen to other people. You have to listen to yourself. I learned a big lesson. Now I don't listen to what other people say about me. I just listen to what I have to say about me."

Andrew age 14

Many boys struggle with self-esteem at your age. You're going through a lot of changes and taking on new social worlds. So it's normal to be uncertain about where you fit in and where you can find other people who value you. Seeing images of "ideal guys" in the media—guys who are athletic, cool, popular, smart, and funny—can also make you feel like you don't measure up in some way. Remember, you always have a choice about what you think and how you feel. You can always raise your self-esteem just by being aware and trying!

Other People and Your Self-Esteem

How much should you let other people's opinions influence your self-esteem? That is a tricky question. On one hand, it builds your self-esteem when someone you respect praises you and shows you that your contributions are valuable. How we feel about ourselves is often mixed with how we think others feel about us. Everyone wants to feel accepted and respected. On the other hand, there are situations when listening to the opinions of others can be damaging and unhelpful. Not everyone's opinion is worth listening to! At the most fundamental level, self-esteem is something you can't get from someone else. You have to give it to yourself.

"Self-esteem is hard to explain to preteens. I think most guys struggle with self-esteem at one time or another. The lesson I learned is this: It does not matter what anyone else thinks about you. In life, all that matters is what you think about yourself, and we are all in total control of that. Self-esteem is a journey, and as we travel through life we can continue to improve our self-esteem, even if we are 100 years old!"

—Cynthia, mother of two

How Do I Deal with Bullies?

Sometimes **bullying** happens without a person even knowing it. You might even have been a bully yourself without meaning to be. Bullying includes physical fights between two or more people, but teasing and name-calling can be forms of bullying, too. Excluding a person from a group can be a form of bullying, as can spreading rumors (things that are not true or that are private or hurtful) about someone. Bullying can happen in-person or through text messages, through email, or on the Internet. All of these forms of bullying should be taken seriously. You do not have to put up with bullying as part of growing up. Many states now have laws about bullying, and schools are required to enforce those laws and to educate their students about bullying.

What can you do if someone is bullying you?

Here are some approaches you might try:

- Avoid or ignore the bully. If you have to, get yourself to a safe place.

- Try not to show how upset the bully makes you. This is part of what keeps bullies going. You can talk about it later to an adult.

- Calmly but firmly tell the bully to stop bothering you. This shows the bully you aren't scared, and it can feel good to stand up for yourself.

- Get help from friends. It's harder to pick on someone who has friends around.

- Get help from an adult. Do not hesitate to do this, especially if you've tried other ideas, but they aren't working.

- Never blame yourself for being bullied—it isn't your fault.

- If someone is bullying you online or on a cell phone, get help from an adult. Show the adult the messages or texts before you delete them.

Dr. H says: "Take responsibility for your well being by being active and getting yourself help if you need it, or use your courage and self-esteem to stand up for yourself."

Look at Yourself

Take a good, hard look at your own behavior. Do you ever bully others? People who bully others often feel insecure about something. If you have bullied someone, think about how you were feeling at the time and how you felt afterward. Counselors and teachers can help you find better ways of dealing with your feelings.

Who You Are Is Important

Remember you are totally, one hundred percent unique! There is no one else in the world exactly like you! You are a special individual with talents and gifts that are yours

Quick Quiz

- You say mean things to other kids on purpose. True or False?
- You pick fights with kids who seem weak or shy. True or False?
- You write text messages or emails that are hurtful or cruel. True or False?
- You tell lies about other kids. True or False?

If you answered "True" to any of these questions, you may be bullying others. Talk to your parents or a counselor for ideas on why you are treating other kids this way. Get help changing your behavior. You can also make changes on your own by deciding you won't treat others this way anymore!

alone. Be proud of your strengths and talents. You have valuable contributions to give the world. Also remember to be grateful for your efforts and your mistakes. Often, you can learn just as much about yourself from your mistakes as you learn from your successes. We all make mistakes. Meeting the challenge and trying is what matters most!

EXERCISE YOUR Self-ESTEEM

- **Make a list of some of the qualities you value in yourself and things that make you feel proud.** Don't be shy! Now is the time to build that strong foundation, so when a storm blows in you can stand strong.

- **Ask friends what they value about you.** Be sure to return the favor and tell them what you appreciate about them!

- **Think about areas where you can improve your self-esteem.** For example, do you feel you don't do well enough in your schoolwork? Do you worry you don't have enough friends? Do you think you should be better at sports? Just because there is something you might like to change about yourself doesn't mean you have less value as a person. Remind yourself of that, and discuss it with an adult you trust. Come up with a plan to improve your self-esteem in each area you'd like to improve. For example, if you want to do better in school, maybe you need to get a tutor in a particular subject, or maybe you can study an extra half hour every night. Make a plan and see how it goes!

- **Try doing something to help someone else.** Not only will this make you and the person you help feel good, but it is also a great way to build self-esteem.

alone, be proud of your strengths and talents. You have valuable contributions to give the world. Also, remember to be grateful for your efforts and your mistakes. Often, you can learn just as much about yourself from your mistakes as you learn from your successes. We all make mistakes during the challenge and trying is what matters most.

School

Let's discuss school...

- How Do I Manage New School Stresses?
- How Do I Improve in School?

How Do I Manage New School Stresses?

At your age, you probably spend more hours at school than any other place besides your home. School can be a lot of fun, but it can also be stressful. Often, when you reach middle school, your workload increases. Sometimes, the pressure to do well and to get things accomplished also increases. In addition, there are other things to balance, like getting along with new teachers, having a locker, and moving from classroom to classroom throughout the day. You might also be involved in sports, music, drama, or other activities after school. Your life is full and busy! Going to your activities, getting your homework done, and getting to bed on time each day can be a real challenge.

You might be experiencing social changes, too. If you're going to a new school, you may need to make new friends. You may start to expand your friendships and perhaps leave some old friends behind. As we talked about in the previous chapter, you will be going through a variety of feelings as you find your way through puberty, and this can make social situations more challenging.

Don't forget the excitement and joy in your life! You will begin to accomplish new things, make new friends, and have new and fun experiences as you grow. All of these happy events take energy!

How Do I Improve in School?

No matter how challenging a subject is for you at school, you can always find a way to improve. Here are some tips:

- Keep a positive attitude.
- Let your teacher know that you want to improve.
- Ask your teacher what he or she suggests so you can get help. Often teachers are happy to spend extra time with you before school or during a study hall.
- Ask your guidance counselor for suggestions.
- Talk to your parents. They may be able to find you a tutor in a subject area that's difficult for you. Sometimes high school or college kids in the area will do this for a very reasonable cost (and sometimes for free).
- Spend extra time going over the subject matter with your mom or dad or even with an older sibling.

Get Organized

Being organized is one the best things you can do to reduce school stress. Here are some helpful ideas:

- Keep a weekly calendar of all your school assignments and after-school activities to help you plan your time each day.

- Use a study calendar to keep track of your assignments and when they are due. Write down everything and cross off assignments as you finish them. Before you go home from school, make sure you have everything you need to complete your assignments.

Dr. H says: "There's almost always something you can do to bring up your grades in a subject, as long as you are willing to work at it. Look at it as a challenge that will improve your self- esteem!"

- Make sure you have an organized way of keeping your assignments, such as a folder for every class.

- At home, have a well-lit, uncluttered, quiet space to use for homework and studying.

- If you have an assignment you are really dreading, promise yourself a little reward when you finish.

- Make sure you start your homework early enough in the evening so you'll be able to finish it without staying up too late.

- Use your organizational skills to make your homework neat and readable.

" I was too embarrassed to tell my teacher I didn't understand what was going on in math class. I kept faking it until I finally got a D on my report card. My dad said I should have told someone, but I didn't know how. Now I have a tutor, and I am doing great in math. I didn't tell anyone I'm getting help, but I wish I'd asked for it sooner."

George age 11

If you need help, ask for it! Start with yourself! Commit to making your best effort to stay organized and reduce your school stress. Besides your teachers, your parents and older siblings may be a great resource to help with a particular subject. Have them quiz you for tests, and listen to their explanations and suggestions. It may also help if you have a study buddy from your class. Plan a time to work together on assignments and to study for tests. You can quiz each other and help each other learn.

Some students need to be tested for learning disabilities—learning challenges that need extra attention. If you need to learn information in a particular way, it does not mean there is something wrong. It simply means you have a special way of processing certain information and you need assistance to learn how best to do that. Some students learn better from reading, others from listening, and still others by just figuring out things for themselves. There are specialists who can help you understand how you learn best, and they can give you the tools to use so you can excel in all your schoolwork.

Dr. H says: "Remember, if you are struggling and stressed, it's important to ask for help. There are all kinds of people and resources available for kids, so that they can do their very best in school!"

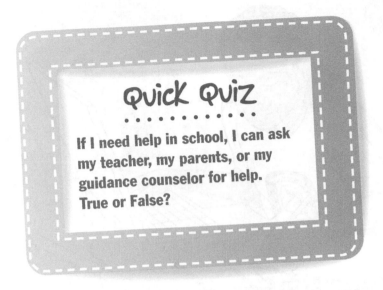

Get Challenged

You may find that some of your classes are too easy. This may cause you to feel bored, unfocused in class, and uninterested in completing assignments. This is a source of stress that you need to address. Here are some ideas for how to handle this:

- **Talk to someone.** Let your teacher or parents know that class is too easy. Sometimes a teacher can give you more challenging books to read or more difficult assignments to complete.

- **Find a tutor.** Tutors who excel in a certain subject can provide more challenging homework and more interesting information than you get in class.

- **Take an advanced class.** Some schools have honors or advanced classes in certain subjects. Ask your teacher or guidance counselor.

- **Look for other opportunities.** Try to find ways to improve your own education and keep it interesting. Go to the library and ask the librarian for suggestions of books to read. Use the Internet to research a chosen topic. There are a lot of fun websites for those who need help or want advanced work!

Focus on Your Strengths

It is important for your self-esteem to focus on your strengths. This is also important for reducing stress. Remember, no one can excel at everything! We all have different strengths and different weaknesses. You may have trouble in English but be a whiz at math. You might be great at track but not at basketball. Praise yourself for whatever you are good at, and ask for help and make a plan for whatever you

want to improve in. Also, remember that it's just as important to be a good friend, to have a good sense of humor, and to be willing to help others as it is to be good at schoolwork. Don't forget to focus on those positive qualities!

Think About School

Take some time to think about school. What, if anything, is causing you stress? If you feel like everything is going well, write down the things that are helping you. For example: You are organized, you have a tutor, you have helpful friends, and so on. If you are stressed about something, write it down and find a trusted adult to help you make a plan to reduce that stress. For example, if you are struggling in math, ask your mom to help you make a plan to improve.

Just For Fun!

17 Friends, Cliques, and Peer Pressure

Let's discuss friends, cliques, and peer pressure

- **How Do I Fit In at School?**
- **How Can I Be a Good Friend?**
- **How Do I Handle Peer Pressure?**

How Do I Fit In at School?

During your preteen and teen years, friendships start to become more important. Your friends and social relationships take on a bigger role in your life as you become more independent from your family. Wanting to fit in with your peers is a normal part of growing up.

Good Cliques

It's common to form deep connections with a small group of people. Such a tightly knit group is often called a **clique** (pronounced "click"). Cliques are not necessarily bad. Good cliques:

- Include friends who really care about you and whom you feel you can talk to about anything.
- Have people who can count on one another for help and to support one another's goals.
- Help make you kind and sociable with a lot of other kids in your class.

Dr. H says: "If your group of friends excludes other people, is mean to others, or forces you to do things or act in ways that you do not like or are uncomfortable with, you may need to think about whether or not this clique is really for you. When you exclude people from your life for no particular reason, you may be missing out on some great friends, and some really fun experiences. It is never a good idea to be mean for any reason."

Bad Cliques

Unfortunately, there can be negative sides to cliques. People in some cliques encourage one another to be mean or stuck-up. They tell you who you can and cannot hang out with. Some cliques gossip or tease a lot. Others might try to pressure you into doing things you don't really want to do. If you begin to feel uncomfortable or unhappy with your group of friends, you may need to think about whether it is the right group of friends for you. It may be challenging to leave the group, but you should always have the freedom to choose your friends.

Evaluating Your Clique or Group of Friends

If you think you may need some new friends, ask yourself if your clique likes you for who you really are. Are the people in your clique trying to make you become just like them, or do they allow you to be yourself? Do they have rules about what you can wear, what activities you can or can't do, and which people you are allowed to socialize with? Are your friends trying to get you to become someone you aren't?

> " I have a best friend, but he and I do stuff with other kids, too. We've known each other since preschool, so I know we will always be best friends."
>
> Dillon   age 11

If the answer to most of those questions is yes, then you may need some different friends. It can be a challenge to leave a clique and change friends, but don't be afraid to do it if you feel it is the right thing. Part of growing up is learning to make hard choices, especially when they are the right choices! You can always ask your parents or another trusted adult for help or advice, too.

Other Relationships

If you choose to be part of a clique, be sure you don't let the clique keep you from exploring other relationships and friendships outside the group. If your friends don't allow you to socialize with anyone outside your group, you will not only miss out on meeting a lot of interesting and fun people but you will also be allowing other people to make decisions for you. Neither of those things is healthy for you.

There is no reason you have to be part of a clique to be happy. What will make you happy is having friends who accept you for who you are and who support your interests and goals. A lot of boys have several close friends, but those friends may not all be close with one another. There's nothing wrong with that.

How Can I Be a Good Friend?

Have you ever heard the saying, "The best way to have a good friend is to be a good friend?" It's true! Friendship is definitely a two-way street. Think about how you treat your friends. Are you a good listener? Do you support your friend if he is going through something hard? Do you ever gossip about him or criticize him behind his back? If you treat your friends the way you would like to be treated, you will eventually have some very good and loyal friends!

The Popular Crowd

It is human nature to want to be liked and accepted. This is especially true during adolescence. At some point, you may notice there's a "popular" group of kids at school.

There's nothing wrong with being a member of a popular group, and there is nothing wrong with not being a member of this group. Sometimes kids are in this crowd because they are super friendly and well-liked by almost everyone. Sometimes kids are in this group for other reasons.

If you are not friends with a popular group of kids, and you really want to be, ask yourself why it is so important to you. It's natural to want to be well liked, but do you want to be friends with a popular group for the right reasons? If being friends with this group does not fit with your interests and values, then maybe it will be better for you not to become a member of this group.

Dr. H says: "Be genuinely friendly and outgoing with all your peers, and you might be surprised by how popular you turn out to be just by being yourself!"

When Friendships Fade

At this stage of your life, you and your friends are going through a lot of changes. You are developing new interests and taking on more adult roles, and so are your friends. In the middle of all this, sometimes old friendships fade and come to an end. Sometimes you are the person who needs more distance from your old friend, and other times you are the one who is left behind. This can bring up a lot of challenging feelings, like sadness and maybe even low self-esteem. But fading friendships are normal both now and when you're an adult. It's important to acknowledge your feelings but also to remind yourself that losing a friend does not mean there is something wrong with you or your old friend. However things work out, you can always enjoy the memories of the time you spent as friends in the past. Focus on the friends you have now, and make room for new friendships in your life, too!

How Do I Handle Peer Pressure?

Even adults are influenced by the behavior and approval of their friends and peer group. Sometimes peer pressure is good! Our peers' influence may help us make all sorts of positive changes in our lives. For example, if you make some friends who enjoy biking, you are more likely to start biking with them. But sometimes friends can influence us in less positive ways. This is usually what people are talking about when they refer to **peer pressure**. Peer pressure happens when you feel like you should do something just because your peers think you should, even when you don't want to or when you know it is wrong.

Most adults have developed a more solid understanding of who they are, and they have more confidence in what they believe, so they are less likely to be influenced by others in negative ways. This is harder at your age. You are just beginning to figure out what you believe, what you feel is right or wrong, and who you are as a person. That's why your friends' opinions influence you more. Again, this isn't necessarily wrong. It is just important for you to be aware of the ways peers influence you. That way you can decide if these influences are positive or negative.

"One of the reasons parents want to keep track of who their kids' friends are is because of peer pressure. Parents want to be sure that their kids are being influenced by their friends in positive ways. A true friend will respect your decisions and wishes and won't pressure you once you've made yourself clear."

—John, parent of two

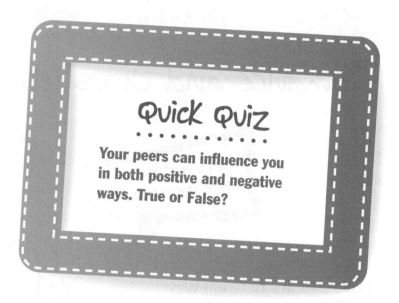

Quick Quiz

Your peers can influence you in both positive and negative ways. True or False?

MAKE A NEW FRIEND

It is wonderful to have a new friend. Maybe someone new moved into your neighborhood or started at your school. Maybe you just started a new activity or joined a new club. Maybe there is someone at school you don't really know, but you would like to get to know that person better. Find your courage, introduce yourself, chat about things you may have in common, eat lunch with this new person, and maybe make a plan to get together after school or on the weekend. Remember, the best way to have a good friend is to be one!

18 Romance and Crushes

- **Why Do I Like Girls in a Different Way Than I Used To?**
- **What About Breaking Up?**

Why Do I Like Girls in a Different Way Than I Used To?

As part of growing up, your feelings about girls may change. When you were younger, you may have thought of girls as just friends, but as you grow up, there may be a particular girl that you begin to have special feelings toward. These feelings are natural and normal, but they may also be new to you. You may be unsure how to handle them. Part of becoming a young adult is learning to understand all your feelings, including romantic ones.

You might also have something called a **crush** on someone. Almost everyone has crushes while growing up. Sometimes the person you have a crush on is someone your age. But a lot of boys get crushes on someone older than them, like an older teen or an adult. You can even have a crush on someone you don't really know, like a movie star or a singer. If you have a crush on someone you know who is your own age, you might want to see if there is a way to spend more time with that person. That way you can find out if you still like that person once you get to know her better.

Going Out

You might notice some boys and girls pairing up with each other. Sometimes this means the couple spends time together at school, or they talk on the phone or text each other. Other times this means the couple does things together outside school, either alone or with a group of friends.

Be sure to talk to your parents to make sure it is okay with them for you to go out with someone special. Some parents might be fine with you spending time with a girl on a group outing, as long as you are supervised by adults. Other parents may not want you to go out with someone you like at all. Be straightforward with your parents about what you want. But be prepared to listen to their thoughts, too.

Remember, if someone does not like you romantically, it does not mean there is something wrong with you. The important thing is to not let it put a big dent in your self-esteem.

Dr. H says: "Sometimes, if you have a crush on somebody, it can be nice to just enjoy the crush. Nobody has to know about it if you don't want them to."

Taking It Slowly

If it's okay with your parents and you do pair up with a girl, remember to take things slowly. Don't get so absorbed with the girl that you forget about your friends, your schoolwork, or your activities. Some couples kiss, but others don't. No one should ever pressure you, and you should never pressure someone else. Trust your instincts and get out of any situation that doesn't feel right.

Some boys aren't ready for this couple stuff at all. That is totally fine, too! There is no reason to rush anything, and there is no right age to become interested in romance. You shouldn't feel pressured into having a girlfriend until you are ready.

Dr. H says: "An important thing to remember as you begin to explore your romantic feelings and crushes is that, like everything in life, there will be ups and downs. Romantic relationships give you the chance to enjoy new people in a new way and learn how to be a good romantic friend and partner. It also teaches you about how to handle hurt, and that's important, too. It is all a part of growing up."

QUick QUiz

If you want to go out with someone special, it is important to talk with your parents about their rules for pairing up and going out.
True or False?

What About Breaking Up?

Sometimes, especially when you're younger, romantic relationships come and go. This might not be a big deal, but it might hurt. It's important to acknowledge disappointed and hurt feelings. But try not to let that be all you think about. Keep busy, hang out with your friends, and do things you enjoy. You may even be able to stay friends with the person you broke up with. Not everybody is going to like you in that special way forever, and it doesn't mean there is anything wrong with you.

If you are breaking up with someone, try to be sensitive about it. Be considerate enough to explain yourself in person. Don't have your friends deliver the message, and don't break up in a text or email. No matter what happens, you will have learned something about yourself, which will help you in future relationships.

Dr. H says: "It is never okay for someone to touch your private parts without your consent. This is called **sexual abuse**, and it is a crime. No one should touch you in a way that makes you feel uncomfortable. Tell an adult right away if this happens to you. It is not your fault, and it is very important that you let a trusted adult know what happened."

Dr. H says: "An important thing to remember as you begin to explore your romantic feelings and crushes is that, like everything in life, there will be ups and downs. Romantic relationships give you the chance to enjoy new people in a new way and learn about how to be a good romantic friend and partner. It also teaches you about how to handle hurt, and that's important, too. It is all a part of growing up and a part of life."

"My first girlfriend broke up with me in an email. I didn't understand why, and she never really explained. I decided I would never do that to someone else. So when I broke up with my next girlfriend, I told her at lunch. She thanked me for not emailing or texting her. It was hard to do in person, but I think it's better."

Andrew age 13

19 Parents

Let's discuss relationships with your parents...

- Why Is It Harder to Get Along With My Parents?
- Do What Is Expected of You

Why Is It Harder to Get Along With My Parents?

Whether you are being raised by your parents, grandparents, or other guardians, you are growing up and taking on increasing amounts of responsibility. You are also becoming more independent. At the same time, you're still rooted in your family life. You still depend on your parents for food, material possessions, advice, and attention. As you push for more independence, it's your parents' job to guide and protect you to make sure you are ready for new responsibilities. There's almost certainly going to be a little friction as you and your parents work through this transition. Your parents aren't trying to be unreasonable. They just have a different perspective and a different job to do than you do.

Good Communication with Parents: Some Basics

There are some general principles that can make communication with parents a little easier.

- **Remember to keep your cool.** It's absolutely fine to get upset about something. But when you are very emotional, it isn't usually the most effective time to communicate. Yelling, slamming doors, or name-calling isn't likely to get you what you want. Most likely it will make things worse. Take some time to cool off and then explain what is bothering you. If you are in the middle of a discussion, and it starts to get heated, tell your parents you need to take a break. Come back when you are able to communicate more calmly.

- **Listen.** Often your parents have insights that can help you. Try to be aware of their feelings, too. Also, if you show parents that you care about their concerns and perspectives (even if you don't agree), they are more likely to negotiate with you and listen to *your* thoughts, too.

- **After you've listened, explain your own position calmly.** Try to help your parents see the situation from your perspective by using "I" statements. Try to avoid language that is too extreme, like the words "always" and "never." For example, say, "I feel like you don't let me hang out with my friends enough," instead of "You *never* let me hang out with my friends."

- **Act like an adult.** If you can act respectfully toward your parents, they are more likely to see you as capable of handling more responsibility. Accept their final decision gracefully, even if it isn't what you wanted. Remember, as you mature, your parents might have a different perspective on the issue.

- **Pick your battles.** Don't argue over every rule or every decision your parents make. Rather, pick those that are most important to you. If you argue about everything, you will simply make your life (and your parents' lives) miserable. Your parents won't be able to tell what really matters to you. You are more likely to get what you want in a specific instance if you don't fight about every little thing.

- **Be ready to negotiate.** Sometimes you and your parents can come to an agreement that has some of what you want and some of what they want. Be open to compromise. If you make a compromise, make sure you live up to your end of the bargain.

Do What Is Expected of You

In general, parents are more likely to give you more privileges when they see you are ready to handle these privileges. This happens over time when you consistently follow rules and do what you are supposed to do without complaint. If you haven't been doing your homework or chores and have been rude to your parents all week, it's unlikely your parents will let you go to a late movie with your friends. Doing what is expected of you helps build your parents' trust. Family rules differ when it comes to dating, chores, curfew, phone privileges, and a lot of other topics. Respecting the rules of the house puts you in a stronger position to negotiate.

> "I made the mistake of yelling at my dad one day when he said I couldn't go to the movies with a group of guys and stay out until 11:00 p.m. After I spent some time in my room, my dad came in and said that my behavior proved to him that I wasn't ready for the responsibility of staying out late. He said when I showed responsibility, I would be rewarded. Now I get it and I am working hard to earn his trust."
>
> Hector age 13

Let Them In on the Details

Letting your parents in on the details of your life helps build trust as well. When you were a little kid, you probably told your parents everything. Now that you are older, you may want to have more privacy. That is normal! But parents need to know some information about your life. It's reasonable for them to want to know what's going on at school, with friends, and with extracurricular activities; what your mood is; and where you're going and what you'll be doing at a certain time. Giving your parents the information they need to keep you safe and guide you will help you build trust, which will likely result in greater independence.

Keep Asking Parents for Advice

Keep asking for your parents' advice and perspective. Your parents have important life experiences they can share with you. They have made mistakes along the way and learned from them, and they can share what they have learned with you. You will likely learn a lot from your parents if you are willing to listen. Even if you listen to their advice, you will probably still make some mistakes. Everyone makes mistakes. It's part of growing up.

Prove It

Remember, your parents may not always know how best to react to your needs. One minute you may act more like a kid, and the next minute you may act quite grown up. This can make it challenging for parents to know how much independence you are really ready for. Show them you are ready to be more independent by sticking to the rules, listening, and communicating. Prove to them you are becoming more and more responsible. That's the best and easiest way to gain more independence and privileges.

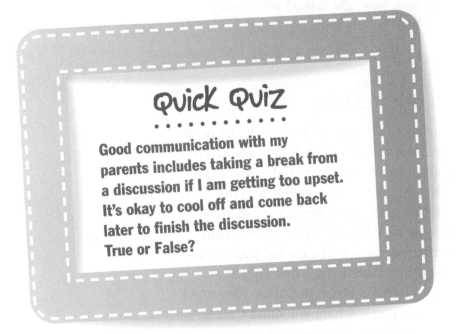

Quick Quiz

Good communication with my parents includes taking a break from a discussion if I am getting too upset. It's okay to cool off and come back later to finish the discussion.
True or False?

Going Through Puberty • A Boy's Manual for Body, Mind & Health

20 Discovering Who You Are

Let's talk about discovering who you are...

- Who Do I Want to Be?
- How Do I Set Goals for Myself?

Who Do I Want to Be?

It may be hard to understand right now, but the choices you make every day direct your life and shape the person you are becoming. The cool thing about being human is that we can always choose to change. This is a great time to begin making choices about the kind of person you want to be. It really is up to you! It is a wonderful and sometimes overwhelming idea, but to a large extent, you really get to choose the person you want to be. You don't get to choose your eye color or whether your hair is naturally curly or straight, but you have a lot of control over the attitudes you take and the choices you make.

As you mature, you'll start to form your own opinions about a variety of topics. Instead of just accepting everything your parents say, you may start to look at things from multiple perspectives. You may start to have different ideas about how things should be done. This can lead to some confusion. You'll be learning all sorts of new things about the world, and you may not like everything you see. During this time of your life, it's natural to question long-held beliefs and opinions. Developing your own beliefs and opinions will help you learn more about yourself and what's important to you.

Developing Your Own Beliefs

Your preteen and teenage years are a natural time to question your beliefs. Part of becoming an adult is developing your own belief system. Developing your beliefs takes time. It doesn't happen all at once. You'll build your beliefs piece by piece, and you'll change your mind about some things as you go. You may not know what you think or feel about a lot of things for a while. That's okay! Start by listening to your own thoughts and those of others. Try to be respectful of others' beliefs, even if you disagree with them.

Try Something New

One of the best ways to learn about yourself is by trying something you've never done before. Trying something new builds your self-esteem and helps you realize your strengths! You may end up doing some of the new things you try for the rest of your life. Some things you may try once and never do them again. This is part of exploring the world. So don't be afraid to try new things!

Dig Deeper

This is also a great time to explore interests you already have even further. You are smarter and more mature than you used to be, which makes interests you already have more exciting. For example, if you really love playing the piano, maybe now you can get more serious about it and practice for competitions. If you already love to cook, you could take cooking classes and learn to prepare new foods. If you enjoy running, swimming, or playing a sport, you might consider trying out for a school team or a traveling team. For every activity, there is always a new, richer layer to explore.

   If you no longer enjoy an activity you've been doing for a while, try talking to your parents about it. They might support you taking a break from it if they know there's another activity you'd like to try instead.

Your Social Self

Part of figuring out who you are happens through your friendships. You might begin to partly define yourself by who your friends are and what you do together. Your friends will start to influence the beliefs you form about the world, and you will influence theirs.

   Many of your relationships with your peers will change a lot during these years. You may be friends with a group of boys for a year, but then realize you don't enjoy hanging out with them as much as

Dr. H says: "This is a perfect time to pick up new activities or to explore a deeper layer of something you already enjoy. These interests may eventually help you choose your career, or they may grow into lifetime hobbies. Many adults lack the time to pursue multiple interests, so take advantage of this opportunity now!"

you used to. This change isn't always easy to deal with, but it is to be expected. You are changing a lot, and your friends are, too. It's best to keep an open mind about yourself and about other people in your life. Remember, you aren't defined by any single relationship in your life. Your social self is just part of who you are.

"As you grow and explore your world, remember that what matters most is not accomplishing a goal, but having the courage to try! It is the trying that counts, no matter what the outcome is."

—Mary, mother of one

Quick Quiz
. . . .

Get a piece of paper and fill in the blanks in the following statements:

1. One thing I really love to do is _____.

2. One new thing I really want to try this month is _____.

3. One place I have never visited and really want to see is _____.

4. One person I'd like to get to know better is _____.

5. If I had to choose right now I would be _____ when I grow up.

Learning About the World

A lot of figuring out who you are involves learning about the world around you. Learning more about the lives, customs, beliefs, and political systems of other cultures and countries will influence how you see yourself in the world. As you learn more about the world, you'll be better able to picture how you'd like to fit into it or how you'd like to change it for the better.

Shaping Your Character

Celebrate the power you have to be the person you want to be! Think about what you want your **character** to be. Do you want to be considerate? Confident? Easygoing? Think about the qualities you most admire in yourself. What are they? For example, do you love being helpful to everyone, even strangers? Maybe you want to develop this quality by volunteering in a food pantry or helping raise money for a charity.

Are there things about your character you would like to improve? For example, maybe you tend to be scared of trying new things. (Many of us are like that.) If you think you'd like to be more adventurous, pick something new and try it. Surround yourself with people who will support your efforts.

How Do I Set Goals for Myself?

We can all take little steps toward becoming the kind of person we

How to SET a GOAL:

- **Write down your goal.**
- **Set a timeline to accomplish your goal.** This might be up to you, or it might be set already. For example, if you are trying out for the soccer team, you already know the tryout date. If you want to get better at drawing, you'll have a less-defined timeline. Be realistic when thinking about how long accomplishing your goal will take.
- **Write down the steps you need to take to accomplish your goal.** If your goal is trying out for the soccer team, your steps might include an extra 30 minutes of practice every night, running three extra laps around the track every other day, and practicing ball handling on Saturday and Sunday.
- **Keep track of your progress.** Record the things you accomplish each day, week, or month as you head toward your goal.
- **Tell some trusted friends and adults about your goal and ask them for support.**
- **Even if you don't reach your goal, be sure to congratulate yourself for trying.** That's what matters most.

want to be. The decisions you make now will powerfully shape the kind of adult you become. Don't underestimate your own capability to change and grow. Now that you are older, you can start setting goals for yourself. Setting goals is a great way to give yourself direction, accomplish a task or challenge, and make changes in your life.

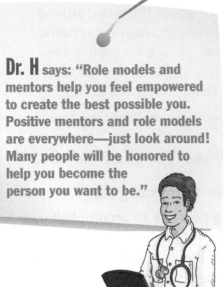

Dr. H says: "Role models and mentors help you feel empowered to create the best possible you. Positive mentors and role models are everywhere—just look around! Many people will be honored to help you become the person you want to be."

Mentors and Role Models

Find as many positive role models and **mentors** as you can. A role model is someone you look up to and admire. A role model might be someone you know well, like a family member, a coach, or a member of your religious community. Because you admire that person, you use his or her life as inspiration for your own life. You can also have role models that you don't know personally, like celebrities. Role models can even be characters in books!

A mentor is someone who takes a more direct role in your life, giving you advice about how to take steps to get where you want to go. If you want to improve your singing, you might tell your music teacher, and he can become your mentor by giving you ideas and supporting your goal.

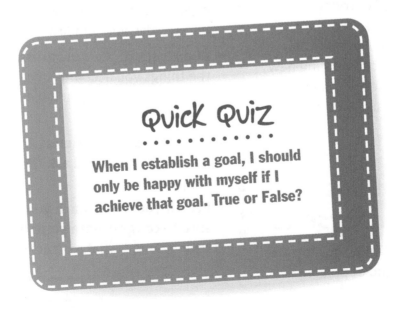

QuiCK QuiZ
· · · · · · · · · · ·

When I establish a goal, I should only be happy with myself if I achieve that goal. True or False?

Enjoy the Ride

As you move through your teen years and become an adult, listen to your inner judgment. You can be your own best friend when it comes to making good decisions and achieving your goals. Remember, you have family members and friends who will always be there for you as you grow and develop. Entering adulthood has its challenges, but it is also a great adventure as you learn, change, and grow. I wish you all the best as you enjoy the ride!

"Guys, you are so lucky to be at this stage in your life where you can try many things and create new goals and dreams. Work hard, have fun, and most of all, appreciate who you are. You can do anything you can dream! Life is what you make it!"

—Ron, father of three

BRAINSTORMING

Set a timer for 15 minutes. Write down all the things you want to try but haven't tried before. Are there places you want to visit? Write them down. Dream big, and then see if there's a way to make your dreams reality, step by step. Choose a dream or goal and make a plan to accomplish it. Talk to your parents about it. The goals can be little, like getting a good grade on your next science test or taking a pottery class. Or they can be big, like visiting all 50 states or becoming a doctor when you're older.

Just For Fun!

Resources

General Health

www.bam.gov

Information and games created by the Centers for Disease Control on diseases, physical activity, safety, making smart choices, and more.

www.kidshealth.org/

Designed for kids, teens, and parents— contains information on puberty, health, dealing with feelings, and more.

http://www.youngmenshealthsite.org/

Created by Boston Children's Hospital, provides information on many health topics for teen boys.

http://pbskids.org/itsmylife/

Includes videos, games, and information for kids on body, emotions, school, family, and friends.

Food, Exercise, and Drugs

Home Strength Training for Young Athletes (DVD-ROM) by Dr. Jordan Metzl. Resource for preteens and teens on beginning strength training produced by the American Academy of Pediatrics.

www.thecoolspot.gov

Provides information on alcohol and resisting peer pressure.

www.teens.drugabuse.gov

From the National Institute on Drug Abuse, provides facts on drugs and activities for teens.

Bullying, Stress, and Self-Esteem

www.stopbullying.gov

Interactive games to help kids understand and prevent bullying. Includes information for adults as well.

The Stress Reduction Workbook for Teens: Mindfulness Skills to Help You Deal with Stress by Gina Biegel (Instant Help, 2010). Contains activities that help young people reduce and manage their stress.

Glossary

A

Acne
A common skin condition that occurs when the pores of the skin become clogged with oil, dead skin cells, and bacteria; it typically includes blackheads, whiteheads, or pimples on the face, chest, or back.

Adolescence
The period including and following the onset of puberty, during which a young person develops from a child into an adult. It also includes maturation of thoughts, feelings, and behaviors.

Androgens
A special group of hormones especially important for male development and reproductive functions. Testosterone is an important androgen.

Antiperspirant
A product used to decrease body odor that contains a substance (aluminum), which decreases the amount of sweat released onto the skin.

Anus
An opening from which feces (poop) exit the body.

B

Benzoyl peroxide
An ingredient that works to kill the bacteria associated with acne formation.

Bullying
Using superior strength or influence to intimidate someone, typically to force him or her to do what you want.

C

Carbohydrates
Nutrients found in starchy foods, such as whole-grain breads, rice, bran muffins, potatoes, sweet potatoes, and pasta.

Character
The mental and moral qualities of your personality that define what kind of a person you are.

Circumcision
A procedure in which the foreskin is surgically removed to expose the end of the penis.

Clique (pronounced "click")
A small group of people with shared interests who spend time together and sometimes exclude others.

Corona
Ring around the base of the glans; part of the penis.

Crush
Intense feelings of liking someone or being attracted to someone, usually not long lasting.

D

Deodorant
A product that has components that cover up body odor; may also contain ingredients that help inhibit the growth of bacteria, which decreases odor.

E

Ejaculation
Muscle contractions that cause the semen to exit out the urinary opening of the penis.

Epididymis
Part of the structure of ducts from which sperm leave the testicles.

Erection
The firm and enlarged condition of the penis when the erectile tissue surrounding it becomes filled with blood, making it stiff.

Estrogens
A special group of hormones especially important for female development and reproductive functions.

F

Fats
Nutrients found in foods like butter, olive oil, canola oil, and margarine.

Foreskin
Extra layer of skin covering the penis found in uncircumcised males.

G

Glans
Bulbous-shaped part at the end of the penis.

Growth spurt
A period of rapid growth.

H

Hair follicle
A "tunnel" lined with skin cells that usually contains a hair and opens to the skin.

Hormones
Signaling molecules made by your body that travel through the bloodstream to the cells of the body, helping control how the cells work.

J

Jockstrap
Type of athletic supporter.

L

Larynx
The voice box. It is responsible for producing speech and contains the vocal cords.

M

Mentor
A person who is an expert in an area that interests you and who takes on the active role of helping you reach your goals in this area.

Mood swings
Extreme or rapid changes in mood.

N

Nocturnal emission (wet dream)
When a boy ejaculates while sleeping.

Nutrients
Chemical substances found in food that your body needs to survive and thrive.

O

Orgasm
A very pleasurable sensation that occurs during ejaculation.

P

Peer pressure
Pressure from one's peers (friends) to behave a certain way.

Penis
An organ that is part of the male reproductive system; contains the urinary opening, which is where semen and urine exit the body.

Pimple (zit)
A type of acne with an inflamed, raised region of the skin that's sore to the touch.

Proteins
Nutrients found in foods like meat; nuts; dairy products like milk, yogurt, and cheese; eggs; and beans.

Puberty
A normal phase of human development that occurs when a child's body transitions into an adult's body and becomes capable of reproduction.

Pubic hair
Hair that grows in the area of the penis and testicles.

R

Razor bumps
Irritated, painful bumps that occur after shaving.

Razor burn
An irritating rash that appears a few minutes after shaving.

S

Salicylic acid
An acne treatment that helps prevent clogged hair follicles and unclog already-clogged follicles.

Scrotum
The loose bag of skin beneath the penis; contains the testicles and the epididymis.

Sebaceous glands
Glands associated with hair follicles that make an oily product called sebum.

Sebum
An oily substance released by the sebaceous glands, which flows up from the hair follicle and out onto your skin or hair, creating increased oiliness.

Self-conscious
Excessively aware of being observed by others; feeling socially uncomfortable.

Self-esteem
Respect for oneself; having a favorable, positive view of oneself.

Semen
Fluid that is ejaculated; it contains sperm and special fluids that help the sperm survive inside a woman.

Sexual abuse
When someone touches someone else's private parts without consent.

Shaft
The main part of the penis that includes most of the penis's length.

Sperm
Special cells found only in males that provide half the genetic instructions needed to make a new baby.

Spontaneous erection
An erection that occurs involuntarily, even when a boy or man is not sexually excited.

Stress
Physical or psychological tension.

T

Testicles (testes)
The male reproductive organs contained within the scrotum; they produce androgens and sperm.

U

Urinary opening
In boys, an opening at the tip of the penis for urine (or semen) to leave the body.

V

Vitamins and minerals
A group of nutrients found in fruits and vegetables and in some other foods.

W

Wet dream (nocturnal emission)
When a boy ejaculates while sleeping.

More Great Books from the
What Now? Series!

Lesson Ladder is dedicated to helping you prepare for life's most fundamental challenges. We provide practical tools and well-rounded advice
that help achieve your goals while climbing the personal or professional
ladder—whether it is
preparing to start a family of your own or getting your child potty trained.

I'm Having a Baby! Well-Rounded Perspectives
Collective wisdom for a more comforting and "balanced" understanding of
what to expect during pregnancy, childbirth, and the days that follow.
$19.99

I Had My Baby! A Pediatrician's Essential Guide
to the First 6 Months
Gain confidence to experience the true joy of parenthood! From learning what to expect during those first minutes in the hospital through your
baby's first 6 months, this concise, reader-friendly, and reassuring guide
covers core topics you'll need to know as a new parent.
$16.99

Making Kid Time Count for Ages 0-3: The Attentive
Parent Advantage
Whether you're a working or stay-at-home parent, this book shows you
how to maximize your time with your baby or toddler with tips for developing a strong parent-child relationship, and ways to ensure strong cogni-
tive, social, and
emotional development for your child.
$16.99

I'm Potty Training My Child: Proven Methods That Work
Respecting that children and parenting styles differ, we created this guide
to offer a variety of effective training solutions to help today's busy parents
with easy, fast reading, and even faster results!
$12.99

Better Behavior for Ages 2-10: Small Miracles That Work
Like Magic
For the harried parent, this book offers the compassion, help, and proven
solutions you need to manage—and preven—difficult child behavior.
$16.99

Call toll-free to order! **1-800-301-4647**
Or order online: **www.LessonLadder.com**

CPSIA information can be obtained at www.ICGtesting.com
Printed in the USA
LVOW02s1707260913

354292LV00002B/2/P